⊰[LOVE RULES]⊱

LOVE RULES

A STUDY OF THE TEN COMMANDMENTS

Christina Hergenrader

CONCORDIA PUBLISHING HOUSE · SAINT LOUIS

This book is for the women who shared their stories—
Jen, Marcilee, Mom, Barb, Bonnie, Amy, Aunt Katie, Lindy,
Judy, Anne, Connie, and Sarah;
and especially for Amanda and Melissa.
Thank you for two years of editing, listening, praying, and reading.
Without you, these pages would still be a binder on my bookshelf.

Published by Concordia Publishing House
3558 S. Jefferson Avenue, St. Louis, MO 63118-3968
1-800-325-3040 · www.cph.org

Text © 2016 Christina Hergenrader

Manufactured in the United States of America

1   2   3   4   5   6   7   8   9   10   25   24   23   22   21   20   19   18   17   16

And God spoke all these words, saying,

"I am the LORD your God, who brought you out of the land of Egypt, out of the house of slavery.

"You shall have no other gods before Me.

"You shall not make for yourself a carved image, or any likeness of anything that is in heaven above, or that is in the earth beneath, or that is in the water under the earth. You shall not bow down to them or serve them, for I the LORD your God am a jealous God, visiting the iniquity of the fathers on the children to the third and the fourth generation of those who hate Me, but showing steadfast love to thousands of those who love Me and keep My commandments.

"You shall not take the name of the LORD your God in vain, for the LORD will not hold him guiltless who takes His name in vain.

"Remember the Sabbath day, to keep it holy. Six days you shall labor, and do all your work, but the seventh day is a Sabbath to the LORD your God. On it you shall not do any work, you, or your son, or your daughter, your male servant, or your female servant, or your livestock, or the sojourner who is within your gates. For in six days the LORD made heaven and earth, the sea, and all that is in them, and rested on the seventh day. Therefore the LORD blessed the Sabbath day and made it holy.

"Honor your father and your mother, that your days may be long in the land that the LORD your God is giving you.

"You shall not murder.

"You shall not commit adultery.

"You shall not steal.

"You shall not bear false witness against your neighbor.

"You shall not covet your neighbor's house; you shall not covet your neighbor's wife, or his male servant, or his female servant, or his ox, or his donkey, or anything that is your neighbor's."

Exodus 20:1–17

{[TABLE OF CONTENTS]}

"1 am the LORD your God, who brought you out of the land of Egypt, out
of the house of slavery."

—God in Exodus 20:2

I REALLY DIDN'T WANT TO WRITE THIS BOOK. When I first started studying the Ten Commandments, a book about them sounded horrible. I worried
it would be a letter to women that read, "Hello. You are not good enough.
Amen."

There is not a single woman in the world who needs that message.

But as I understood more about the Ten Commandments, I realized I had
them all wrong. The Commandments show us how to live with God and
with one another. We look to them for direction and perspective. They give us
boundaries. The Commandments are where we look for our value, for love, for
our identity as God's people.

Or more accurately, where we should *not* look.

The idea that God warned us about all this thousands of years ago intrigues
me. Really? And are we *still* stubbing our toes in the same ten spots today?

So I started to write my stories and my friends' stories of our most painful
seasons, about the times we've looked for love and security and value in all
the wrong places. I've collected forty stories. And yep. These stories are about
how we still believe the same lies God warned us against in Exodus when He
etched the Ten Commandments into stone.

We have trusted the world's bad advice and thrown ourselves into disastrous
relationships. We've devalued the sacred and valued what we could buy with
our credit cards. These are the stories about how we have worked tirelessly

seven days a week so we can consume way more than we want or need.

God designed us for so much more than this. We are His holy people, set apart. We belong to Him, not to the world. He never wanted us to find our value in work, in things, or in whether people like us.

Understanding this has been like putting on a new pair of glasses. Maybe this is why God told us to write the Ten Commandments on our hearts. Because they are a love letter to us, His people: "Dear ones, you are good enough *because I love you.* Amen."

At the heart of that letter is Jesus. Because of Jesus and His love, we are valuable, fully accepted, totally pleasing to God. The longing for this value is at the core of every one of our stories. God loves us so much that He rewrites our stories to be testaments of His love.

And now, these are the stories we get to share with the world.

Amen?

Amen.
CHRISTINA

P.S. I've changed some of my friends' names in this book. *Love Rules* is supposed to be the furthest message from condemnation, and some of these stories are about the worst decisions the people I love have made. You'll recognize the stories as true, but identifying information has been changed.

Don't Have Other Gods

"You shall have no other gods before Me."

—God in Exodus 20:3

One of them, a lawyer, asked [Jesus] a question to test Him. "Teacher, which is the great commandment in the Law?"

And He said to him, "You shall love the Lord your God with all your heart and with all your soul and with all your mind. This is the great and first commandment."

—Jesus in Matthew 22:35–38

THE BAD NEWS is that God starts the Ten Commandments with the hardest one of all. The good news is that this commandment is at the heart of the other commandments. If you could just follow the First Commandment, you could close this book. The First Commandment is, as Jesus said, the greatest commandment of the Law.

But none of us can pull off the First Commandment. Our hearts are idol factories, churning out worship for a conveyor belt of shiny objects and promises. We worship the power that comes with success, the comfort money gives us, the security in relationships, and our own ability to get stuff done.

The good (bad?) news is that this misguided worship is nothing new. Thousands of years ago, when God gave the Israelites the Commandments, He knew they had some big moments coming up: Jericho's impossible walls, the weeks of no meat, the treacherous trek to the Promised Land. God's people had a choice: They could either trust themselves or trust Him. They could watch His plan of redemption unfold through tumbling walls, satisfying manna and quail, and crazy-good love, or they could worship a calf they had made from their own gold jewelry.

This is our choice too. We won't be any more satisfied with these golden calves than our ancestors were. And although our minds know this, our hearts can't stop worshiping them. We believe that Jesus is a true Savior, yet we want something we can hold in our hands.

The way you see the rest of the commandments, how you see your life, depends on how you answer this first question: Who do you really trust will take care of you?

THOUGHTS ABOUT THIS COMMANDMENT

1. To explain the First Commandment, Martin Luther says, "We should fear, love, and trust in God above all things." He begins his explanation of each commandment with "We should fear and love God," but he adds "trust" to this one. Why?

2. Maybe it's the "above all things" in the explanation of the First Commandment that's hardest for us. What other things do you trust more than God? In the stories on the following pages, we'll look at women who have trusted money, friends, and their own abilities more than God. What about you? What other things do you trust above God?

1 Roots

"Blessed is the man who trusts in the LORD, whose trust is the LORD. He is like a tree planted by water, that sends out its roots by the stream, and does not fear when heat comes, for its leaves remain green, and is not anxious in the year of drought, for it does not cease to bear fruit."

—God in Jeremiah 17:7–8

AS WOMEN, WE HAVE BLACK-BELT RELATING SKILLS. We can empathize, connect, bond, and love so well; we may find our value in our friends. When it comes to relationships, we often turn good friends into gods.

What's your story about finding your identity in another person? Maybe it was your first boyfriend, a college roommate, sister, or your very best friend. You loved, protected, worshiped, and leaned on this one person—until your relationship developed stress fractures. If your story is anything like mine, that friendship buckled under the weight of your expectations.

At seventeen years old, I started college in Nebraska. I was eight hundred miles away from my Texas home, and I was insecure. The first day of college, I met my new best friend, the girl who would be my security, my plumb line, my other half, for the next twenty years.

Through college, Jen and I were inseparable. We took the same courses, worked at the same restaurant, dated boys who were also friends, and zigzagged the United States on road trips. We shared clothes, our deepest secrets, a car, a last name, and the same opinion on just about everything.

The cult of our friendship was the soil in which we planted ourselves. All my life I had wanted to belong like this. We rearranged our class schedules to eat lunch together, and we rearranged our lives to spend holidays together.

Right after graduation, Jen and I went dateless to a wedding and met the men who would eventually be our husbands. They had been friends for years. Perfect.

Mike and I married quickly and moved to Houston. Jen also moved to Houston and got a job teaching in the classroom next to mine. Meanwhile, she planned her wedding to Kenny. We started grad school together and again took all the same courses. Even grown-up life couldn't change our story of togetherness.

Until everything did change.

Early one morning, on what would become one of our most terrifying mornings, Jen called in a panic. A man had broken into her apartment, put a pillowcase over her head, and assaulted her. We were twenty-four years old and suddenly living a nightmare we didn't think could happen to nice girls like us.

When I showed up at her apartment, Jen was bloody, bruised, and in terrible shock. I drove her to the ER. (We should have called an ambulance, but we were too dazed to think.) We kept asking each other, "How had this man gotten through the locked doors? Who was he?"

It felt like someone had picked up the snow globe of our lives and smashed it into a million sharp fragments. Nothing was secure. As I was helping Jen figure out where she would live, I was too scared to say what my brain was processing—the new idea that nothing was really safe.

Jen spent the next few days in ICU for a bruised liver. Meanwhile, she talked to a constant stream of police officers and investigators. She filled out reports and tried to piece together what had happened.

When she was released from the hospital, the police still had not found her attacker. The idea that he was still out there—maybe watching her—kept us panicked. We moved truckloads of furniture and photo albums out of her apartment and put most of her things into storage. Jen and her cat moved into the tiny spare bedroom of the townhouse Mike and I had just bought.

She didn't know what to do next. Go to work? See a counselor? Pray? She couldn't sleep and needed Mike or me near her to feel safe. She was moody and scared and trying to figure out why God had let this happen. She was fighting hard spiritual battles, and I had no weapons to give her. And I missed *us*. With my friend incapacitated by fear and trauma, I didn't know who I was.

Life was shifting around us, and we became agitated with each other. Jen's hurt was deeper than our intertwined roots could reach. She needed something nourishing, and it wasn't me. Even though I realized I was letting Jen down, that I would probably ruin the best friendship of my life, I shut her out. I didn't go to counseling with her or pray with her. I buried myself in my life as wife and teacher and left Jen alone. While her life was bleeding all over the rug, I was looking the other way.

Over the next few months, we were constantly annoyed with each other. The day she moved out to live with another family, we didn't say a word to each other. Resentment brewed between us, and neither of us knew who to blame.

Our friendship was supposed to be an ironclad, gold-standard, never-fail loyalty. Except it wasn't. When the worst-case scenario happened, I couldn't provide more than superficial help, and I couldn't heal her. But God could do all that. During the next year, Jen would get to know her Savior better than ever before.

Even though Jen has loved God her whole life, this is where she learned her firsthand stories of redemption. She recognized that He was with her through every step of that hard season, always soothing her and igniting her faith. He turned her terror into strength. I see that strength all the time, especially in her steely determination to share her faith with her two young daughters and son.

I wish I could see Jen more often, but our lives are too separate nowadays. I quit teaching to become a writer. Mike and I moved to the other side of Houston. Slowly, and sometimes all at once, our interests and friendship circles divided into new ones. We excavated our root systems from each other. It hurt a lot. I still miss our oneness. I miss being half of a duo.

My eleven-year-old, Catie, has a new friendship that is similarly intense. She and her BFF have inside jokes and their own secret language, and they are hurt when the other one eats lunch with someone else. They are fiercely loyal to each other. They also spend a lot of time disappointed by each other; they fight, make up, cling to each other, and repeat.

By watching Catie and her friend, and by looking back on my friendship with Jen, I can see that our human relationships just can't handle that kind of pressure. God never meant for a friend to give us our value. You are not good because your best friend loves you; you are good because Jesus loves you and paid for all your sins on the cross.

Catie and I are having lots of conversations about how a friendship can be good but not a god. We're talking about what a friendship can give and what it can't. Only God can give us the deeper, richer nutrients we really need.

You and I both need these deeper, richer nutrients. We need communion with Jesus, our Savior. We need forgiveness from our Father through His Son, Jesus. We need spiritual fruit from the Holy Spirit.

Only God can fulfill all our expectations, our needs. Only God can handle our worship.

This sweet place of perfect friendship—this is where God roots us. *This* is where He wants us to grow.

YOUR STORY/GOD'S STORY

1. Like most of us, you've probably relied on a relationship—your first serious boyfriend, first best friend, your husband, or your mom—to fill a hole inside yourself. Tell your story about when another person has become your god.

2. What does God want relationships to provide for you, and what can they not? Explain.

3. Read Matthew 10:30–33. Talk about your identity as God's daughter. What does it mean that He loves you, provides everything you need, and doesn't want you to be afraid? Can you tell a story that shows this?

4. What are the nutrients God provides that you desperately need? Be specific here. List the ways God has taken care of you this week, this month, this year. How are those the nutrients that keep you close to Him?

5. If you struggle to trust God above all things, are friends one of the main "things" you believe in more than God? Think about your relationships right now. Is there a specific one for which you need God's help to see whether it is a good thing or not a good thing?

PRAY . . .

Lord, You are the only one who can give my soul what it needs.
Root Your love in my heart so that I find my value in You.
Help me to depend on You as my Savior more than I depend on
my friends or family. Thank You for loving me enough to send
Jesus as my Savior. In His redeeming name. Amen.

Super Sam

For I consider that the sufferings of this present time are not worth comparing with the glory that is to be revealed to us.

—Paul in Romans 8:18

FOR MOST OF US, it's easy to trust God during dramatic flashes of terror. Prayer in these moments comes effortlessly, almost as involuntarily as our brain's flight-or-fight hormones.

It's harder to trust God's sovereignty over a long, painful season. It's a more complicated faith to know God is able to heal someone you love but He's choosing not to. These believers trust that God loves them, yet they cannot understand why He isn't answering their most desperate prayers.

This is the case for our friends the Engmans. Nathan is the director of Christian education at our church. He and his wife, Sarah, are smart, quiet, and hardworking. They had been married six years when their son Sam was born. Sarah had been waiting for this moment her whole life. Seriously. Sarah said she had dreamed about becoming a mom from just about the time *she* was born.

As a newborn, Sam was healthy but soon had trouble eating, and his motor skills were lagging. Nathan and Sarah are not dramatic, paranoid people, and they didn't freak out about Sam's slow progress. He was their gorgeous brown-eyed baby, and he was just taking his time learning to control his little body.

But at his six-month checkup, Sarah started to get concerned. Sam didn't meet the pediatrician's milestones. He wasn't sitting up, trying to crawl, or eating and sleeping any better. The doctor reassured them that as long as Sam kept progressing, they shouldn't worry.

When Sam turned one, even calm, rational Sarah was getting scared. Sam's eyes began crossing, his body would suddenly jerk, his immune system struggled to fight off viruses, and he was slipping further and further behind his peers. The Engmans took Sam to a neurologist, but the MRI showed nothing. The Engmans were praying for answers. Was Sam still just developing slowly? Would he always be a little behind his peers?

Sam's ENT doctor suggested removing his adenoids and putting in tubes. Nathan and Sarah thought this might be the help Sam's body needed. Maybe fixing his ear infections would help his overall health.

But after the surgery, Sam regressed. He no longer crawled, he struggled to sit up, and he didn't try to walk. Weeks after the surgery, he was still groggy from the anesthesia. Sometimes he would scream and scream for no reason.

Sarah and Nathan kept praying and looking for answers. They tried changing his diet, sought out multiple doctors, and searched the Internet to find answers. But their questions only led to more questions. What invisible monster was doing this to their son?

Their doctor tested for scary diseases—ones that had no cure. As he would rule out one, he would test for the next one. Sarah said she felt like she was losing her mind. Two years had been a very long time to watch her son struggle without knowing why.

Around the time Sam turned two, his health crisis became much more serious. Nathan had just left for Kenya to serve on our church's mission trip when Sam began having seizure-like symptoms and yelling in pain. He was hospitalized. Nathan was more than twenty-four hours from home, sharing the Gospel with those in scary situations, while his son back home was in a scary situation of his own.

In the months following Sam's release from the hospital, the Engmans received results from their genetic testing. They finally had an answer: Sam was diagnosed with infantile neuronal ceroid lipofuscinosis (Batten disease, for short), a very rare, deadly genetic mutation. Sam's cells don't have the right equipment to remove waste from the cells, and this causes them to deteriorate, mostly in his brain. The symptoms of Batten disease include seizures, blindness, dementia, and muscular issues similar to ALS.

The prognosis was grim. Infantile Batten is very aggressive and always dead-ly. Sam's health would quickly deteriorate. Doctors braced Sarah and Nathan for the intense care their son would need for the rest of his life.

Today, the Engmans' life is both scary and stable. At age 4, Sam is blind, in a wheelchair, fed through a G-tube, and taking several medications. But Sam is so much more than a diagnosis. He loves music and being around other kids. Recently, the Engmans went to Disney World on a Make-A-Wish trip. Sam giggled at the sounds, the music, and the happiness of being with his family.

Sarah and Nathan share Sam with the world, helping to teach kids not to be intimidated by his wheelchair. Everyone at our church calls him Super Sam because he is a tremendous gift to the hundreds of people who know him as a brave, sweet boy fighting for his life.

Perhaps most important, Sarah and Nathan share Sam—and their faith—with the Batten community. Other kids are fighting this horrible disease, and some of their families don't know Christ. Sarah and Nathan share Jesus' love with those in darkness.

Last year, Nathan and Sarah had a second son, Luke. He is one of the most energetic one-year-olds any of us have ever seen. During church, teenagers and old ladies fight over who gets to hold and play with Luke.

Sarah and Nathan are doting parents to both Luke and Sam, to their son who needs constant play and their son who needs constant care. Their perse-verance to provide for both boys is a testament to how they accept and cele-brate the children God has given them.

Sarah and Nathan trust that God will heal Sam when the time is right—either today or when Sam is in heaven. But still, the waiting hurts. Lots of days, Sarah and Nathan have more questions than answers. But because they believe God is the only one who has the power to heal Sam, they trust He is also the one who knows when the perfect time will be to provide that healing, even on the days when this waiting is really hard.

Sarah and Nathan's faith is a miracle. This is the same faith Sam and Luke received through their Baptism. This is the faith the Holy Spirit gives us all in Baptism, the faith we have during the dramatic moments of fear, the difficult seasons of suffering, and the restful moments of knowing who is taking care of us.

YOUR STORY/GOD'S STORY

1. What suffering are you asking God to heal? Share your story. How does He keep you strong, even while you're waiting?

2. When we're scared and not sure about God's timing, our temptation is to rely on ourselves and on what we can control. Talk about how your need to control has kicked dust in your eyes and blinded you to God's timing. What dust from your own scrambling is clouding your vision right now? How has the Holy Spirit cleared the dust from your eyes?

3. God's plan is so much more epic than your own. His vision spans generations that haven't been born, generations to come that you cannot even imagine. God's perfect plan weaves together threads you don't see. Can you think of an example from the Bible that shows how God's plans are always more epic than human plans?

4. Read Ecclesiastes 3:1–15. God always gives you enough light for the next step. He hears your desperate prayers and provides exactly what you need according to His will for you. Talk about how God is the one to trust. What does this mean to you?

5. Luther's explanation of the First Commandment is that we should "fear, love, and trust in God above all things." Think about a particularly hard struggle you have right now. What does it look like to love God more than anything else? What about to trust Him? What about to fear (or obey) Him?

PRAY . . .

Father, Your plan for my life is perfect. Help me to trust that. Lord, comfort me in my suffering. Focus my heart on Jesus and His sacrifice that means I will spend eternity in heaven. In His redeeming name. Amen.

The Beach-House God

"No one can serve two masters, for either he will hate the one and love the other, or he will be devoted to the one and despise the other. You cannot serve God and money."

—Jesus in Matthew 6:24

WE LIVE IN ONE OF THE WEALTHIEST COUNTRIES in the world, which may be one of the reasons we are passionate consumers. We like to buy lots and lots of stuff. Pretty small things, expensive big splurges, useful gadgets that promise to save us time and energy, better cars, and bigger houses.

For me, consumerism reached a new level when we had a chance to buy a second home. Owning a beach house in Galveston, Texas, my hometown, was a bucket-list dream for me. Mike was wary about taking on the extra work and mortgage, but in the end, my enthusiasm won over his doubt, and we bought a little cottage close to the shore.

This victory felt like the single most exciting development in our family's story. We. Were. Getting. A. Beach. House. Hallelujah. Life could now begin.

But to pay for the house, we would have to rent it out when we weren't using it. To rent it out, we'd have to fix it up—and it was in bad shape. Old sand had hardened into a cement-like paste in the corners. Although we had bought the house furnished, the couches and beds were ratty and smelled like they had been stuffed with wet towels.

For the next couple of months, our family dropped out of real life. We drove to Galveston every weekend to haul out old furnishings, carry in Craigslist couches and IKEA rugs, change outdated lighting, paint rooms, and pull up carpet.

"Why?" our kids kept asking. "Why did we buy this house?"

"Why?" our family and friends asked. "Do you have time for this?"

If I were honest, we did not have time for this. But I needed this house like a middle-school girl needs designer jeans. I needed our second-home status to tell the world that our family was worthy and wealthy. I also believed that we needed a second house for the nest egg of security it represented.

Anyone talking to us during those frantic months could tell we could not handle the extra expense or stress. We were spending money and time we didn't have for something we didn't need. The renovation was taking its toll on our family. The kids begged to stay home on weekends to rest. Under the pressure of my bloated dream, Mike and I bickered.

I knew I was running everyone ragged, but instead of thinking about why I needed this house so much, I just moved forward. Buy the new furniture. Paint the cabinets. Stuff the hole inside myself—and don't stop to look at what I was stuffing into that hole.

When the house was almost finished, we invited over a friend I hadn't seen in a long time. His family had just moved to Galveston, and he was one of those people I wanted to impress; I wanted him to believe our family was special.

When he arrived at the house with his wife and two sons, our family was sweaty and tired. I suspected his family was also in a bad place. He had been fired from his job at a Florida high school for not winning enough basketball games. He got a job at a Christian high school where he could coach basketball, but he took a significant pay decrease. They were underwater with their Florida house; their family of four would have to sell it at a loss and move in with his parents. I confess that I felt a little relieved knowing they were in an even worse spot than we were. We might have been in emotional chaos, but they were in financial chaos; he mentioned they might have to declare bankruptcy.

And then he said, "We are excited to see how God works this one out."

Wait. What?

No anxiety, no fear, no complaining, no freaking out that their bank account was empty. When we asked how we could help, they were totally confident

God would delight them with the next right path. This was the real-life picture of trusting God.

What about me? I trusted in hard work, in quarterly bonuses, in bank accounts, and in stuff I can put in my cart at Target. To solve a problem, to feel better, to feel satisfied, I relied on what I could collect and consume. Money was anesthesia for my restless soul. My value was tethered to new patio sets and cute throw pillows.

Seriously?

As the summer wore on, I began to see that the beach house wasn't going to give me what I had hoped it would. It was turning out to be a good thing, a fun place for our family, but my heart was an idol factory that could make a god thing out of any good thing.

For thousands of years, God has been telling us that the pretty, sparkly stuff won't make us feel better. Not really. He keeps offering His hand to pull us from our sinkholes of stuff. But most of us just buy more, still looking to purchase the peace God offers us for free. Buying the beach house was my hard, expensive lesson about how money can never work as my god. Eventually, it all becomes more things I'm managing, a bigger drain on my time and energy.

I wish I could remember this the next time I find myself in the mall, trying on jeans I can't afford. I wish I would remember how much more loved I feel when I read God's Word. I wish I could hold on to the relief I feel when I confess my sins. When I feel restless, I wish I would remember to pray instead of scrolling Zulily.

My prayer is that the Holy Spirit keeps filling this God-shaped hole in my soul with His love, grace, and forgiveness.

YOUR STORY/GOD'S STORY

1. Read 1 Timothy 6:6–10. Deep down, many women believe one more thing will make her happy. Just the vacation home or the extra $3,000 in the bank or the bigger closet filled with better clothes. Even if you've discovered this isn't true, even if you've found out the hard way that our insecurity itches deeper than money can scratch, we keep trying. How do you see this in your own life?

2. Read Matthew 6:19–21. We live in a tangible world, where we value what we can hold in our hands and what we can buy with our credit cards. If you trust the lie that tangible things will give you true contentment, then what do you start to believe about our intangible God? Are any parts of our faith tangible?

3. Read Philippians 4:19. Paul writes to the Philippians about the tension between trusting the eternal, intangible riches we have through Jesus and our need for money in this tangible world. Where do you see yourself in this tension? Do you find yourself trusting the forever promises of God or the frantic need for more money?

4. Read John 1:9–13. God has already defined you as His daughter. What does this identity mean to you?

5. Really? Fear, love, and trust in God above *all* things? Even money? Think about what your next month looks like. Where are some places you'll be tempted to rely on money for your happiness or security? What can you do to keep your faith in God?

PRAY . . .

Lord, help me to see you as my God, instead of money. Help me to stop putting my faith in what I can save or buy. Fill my heart with Your powerful love, and take away my neediness. Thank You for Jesus and His sacrifice that paid for all my sins. In His redeeming name. Amen.

Mom's Superpowers

But [the Lord] said to me, "My grace is sufficient for you, for My power is
made perfect in weakness." Therefore I will boast all the more gladly of my
weaknesses, so that the power of Christ may rest upon me.

—Paul in 2 Corinthians 12:9

ASK A GROUP OF WOMEN WHO THEY ARE and what their primary focus is,
and most of us will start talking about our kids. We see our role as moms—as
protectors to our defenseless kids—as our most important job. We are so desperate to care for our kids, we feel like we need superpowers. We can't trust
our babies to anyone else—not even to God.

Unless, of course, the unthinkable happens, and God is the only one who
can protect your child. This is the story of when tragedy struck my friend Bonnie. More than that, this is the story of Bonnie's mom, Barb.

Bonnie is the most energetic, confident, fun person I know. Her processing
time between an idea and attacking it is about ten seconds. Let's take a trip!
Try this! Have you heard of that? If it's new, fun, or exciting, Bonnie is the girl
you want along.

Bonnie works as a social worker, but she is also a certified massage therapist.
As a gift to me for my fortieth birthday, she offered massages to my friends.
But the day she was supposed to come, she canceled. "I think I have the flu.
Or food poisoning. I don't feel like myself at all."

She didn't sound like herself either. When I checked in with her later that
week, I learned that she had gone to urgent care and had been given a pre-
scription for an antibiotic.

A few days later, Barb called from the ER. Bonnie was having seizures. She was being admitted into the hospital.

The next week was bizarre and terrifying. Bonnie's memory began to slip. She started having scary manic episodes. Her doctor diagnosed her as extremely psychotic and said she was having a nervous breakdown.

This diagnosis didn't make sense to those of us who knew Bonnie. She was very busy, but she wasn't stressed. She handled responsibility easily. She had been completely fine before the flu symptoms.

In just a few days, Bonnie's health problems progressed from mental to physical. She couldn't eat. Her lungs were filling with fluid. Every part of her body was shutting down. She slipped into a coma. The doctors moved her to ICU.

That same night, a CT scan showed a tumor on Bonnie's ovary. Her neurologist realized her seizures and deteriorating mental state were actually anti-NMDA receptor encephalitis, a rare brain disease. Bonnie's immune system was trying to attack the tumor, but it was attacking her brain instead.

For the next three weeks, Bonnie's family and friends rallied around her. Machines breathed for her, fed her, moved her legs, and hydrated her. We prayed constantly in her room. Other patients progressed out of ICU, but Bonnie got worse. Double pneumonia. Staph infections. No response from her. We kept saying, "She had just been fine. I was just with her. How could this happen?"

We weren't afraid just for Bonnie, although that was most of it. We were also afraid for ourselves. Bonnie's own body had spontaneously turned on her. If this could happen to indestructible Bonnie, each of us was much more vulnerable than we realized. We couldn't protect ourselves, our kids, our friends. Where did that leave us?

Ironically, it was Barb who had been working on this same lesson with me ever since I had become a mom. When I freaked out that my kids had croup, or when I felt helpless over their learning disabilities, Barb prayed with me: *Lord, help me know these kids belong to You. You are in control. Even as their mom, I'm powerless, Lord.*

Now it was Barb's baby who was in a scary situation, and Barb who could have been freaking out. But her faith was unshakable. While I was writing blog entries and CaringBridge sites for Bonnie, Barb was praying. I was Martha, grasping for some chores and some control. Barb was Mary, resting in

Jesus. *Prayer. Breathe. Prayer. Wait. Prayer.*

Every single hour Bonnie was in the hospital, God gave Barb immeasurable peace. Her faith told her it was God, not her mommy superpowers, that would heal Bonnie. I was in awe. If it had been one of my kids in a coma, I would have reduced God to a lucky rabbit's foot. Not only did Barb trust that God would heal Bonnie right now, but she also trusted that this struggle would further His kingdom and help generations yet to come. She trusted her most valuable blessing to God instead of herself.

One day when I was alone with Bonnie in the ICU, she started to convulse, and her blood pressure shot up. This was a seizure and could mean permanent brain damage. I called for the doctor to come, but he wasn't in the wing.

"Please!" I yelled to a woman in scrubs. "Help me. She needs the sedative." But this woman said only a doctor could administer the antiseizure meds.

Bonnie's body stiffened. I yelled for the neurologist. The nurse shouted he was on his way. Totally powerless, I finally prayed. I finally told God I had no idea what was going on, but Bonnie and I needed Him.

At that moment, I understood the peace Barb had. The elephant stepped off my chest as I admitted my own weakness. I felt God everywhere in that hospital room. Bonnie's face relaxed. She, too, was suddenly peaceful. This is the closest I've ever been to an instant miracle, and I will never forget it.

After a couple of months, Bonnie was released from the hospital, and she's now fully recovered. Yes, she has had to relearn everything her brain short-circuited, but she has done it with her trademark sparkle and enthusiasm. Barb has been by her side, celebrating every new day with her.

That feeling of powerlessness has stuck with me, though. So many days, I feel so capable that I'm tempted to tackle the world on my own. Especially when it comes to my kids. I feel like I need to be indestructible for them. I can show no weakness. Protecting them is my honor and my job.

But then I remember Barb and the gift of her helplessness in ICU. I see my own fragility—even as a mom—clearly. Life is a hurricane, and I'm in the center of it, holding a broken umbrella, hoping it will protect me. I'm not indestructible, and I am not a superhero. I'm defenseless, and so are my kids. We need a real Savior.

I think of Paul's words in 2 Corinthians 12:9, finally admitting it's okay to be weak. In my weakness, I can see the power of Christ.

In the happiest moments, the scariest ones, and everything in between, Christ *is* true peace. He has offered Himself as a sacrifice for me, as a place to cling, to find real rest.

YOUR STORY/GOD'S STORY

1. When we want to protect those we love, our human weakness never feels like a gift. But with the Holy Spirit, we can look back on our weakest moments to see God's strength. Tell your story about one of your weakest moments.

2. Read John 15:5. God is the source of all life. Picture the illustration in this verse and talk about how perfectly this image shows our total dependence on Him.

3. Sin lies to us and says we only need to be more self-confident, tougher, and harder working to be successful. But this isn't true. Where does independence from God get us?

4. Read Romans 12:3–8. What abilities has God given you to tackle life? How can God-given abilities be good but not gods?

5. The world tells us we should absolutely trust ourselves more than anything else. Talk about how Luther's explanation of the First Commandment, "we should fear, love, and trust in God above all things," conflicts with the conventional wisdom that you should trust your own self-confidence more than you trust God. Going forward, where do you hope to trust God more than yourself?

PRAY . . .

Lord, I am so weak, and Your love is so powerful. Help my heart to delight in Your strength and Your love, which never runs out. Only through Your Son can I be content in my weakness. In His redeeming name. Amen.

COMMANDMENT TWO

Don't Use the Lord's Name in Vain

"You shall not take the name of the LORD your God in vain, for the LORD will not hold him guiltless who takes His name in vain."

—God in Exodus 20:7

"Truly, truly, I say to you, a servant is not greater than his master, nor is a messenger greater than the one who sent him. If you know these things, blessed are you if you do them."

—Jesus in John 13:16–17

IN THE EARLY '90s, AOL launched an advertising campaign showing all the cool ways you could use the Internet. Find a hotel! Email your friends! It was all so exciting that thousands called the 1-800 number to buy the AOL CD that would bring them the Internet.

Except many people didn't understand that the CD worked only in a computer. My friend Leslie's family was angry that they had been tricked. Wait! You have to buy a computer to get the Internet?

The salesman, exasperated, said, "Yes, but now you will have a *computer*!"

I think this shows a little about how we see ourselves as Christians. We love the idea of a powerful God who heals our hurts and forgives our mistakes. But wait! Calling ourselves Christians means actually following Christ? Using His name means a life dependent on Him? Is this a trick? A life worshiping Him means we have to *change*?

I suppose God could say, "Yes, but now you're following Jesus! You're finally on the right track, the only track that will end well!"

When we want to use God's name without living a life dependent on Him, it's like using the software without buying the computer. The Second Commandment makes us ask ourselves, "How do I serve God, and how does God serve me? Do I just want to use His name as a handy tool, or am I willing to let His power change my whole life?"

Your answers to these questions show up in the ways you talk about God. Perhaps you borrow His name to boost your own credibility. Maybe you use His name as a curse word or a way to sound very serious when you make a "swear-to-God" promise. God's name can seem like a potent exclamation mark to anything you say. But when we do this, we disfigure our relationship with God. This is using the software without acknowledging that its power comes from the computer. This is using God's name without acknowledging our dependence on Him.

In the Second Commandment, God tells you that using His name for anything except prayer and praise is using it in vain. God wants you to experience a life of more than just yourself, more than someone who gives you more authority.

God wanted this for the Israelites too. When He gave them the Second

Commandment, they didn't know Him yet. He had said, "I am who I am" (Exodus 3:14), but what did that mean?

Then He revealed, year after year, century after century, His perfect holiness and love. He called them into a life with Him.

God calls us into this life too, even though His holiness and love still awe and confuse us. We see, year after year, what it means to be Christian. Jesus tells us to call on His name because He is our Savior, not because His name makes us look better. He is our Lord who humbled Himself in the ultimate act of service—suffering and death on the cross in our place—and now we are moved to reflect that love toward others.

When we understand this relationship, we tell the world, "He's the teacher, and we are the students. He is the message; we are the messengers. He is the power that changes our whole lives."

THOUGHTS ABOUT THIS COMMANDMENT

1. To explain the Second Commandment, Martin Luther said, "We should fear and love God so that we do not curse, swear, use satanic arts, lie, or deceive by His name, but call upon it in every trouble, pray, praise, and give thanks." How is using the Lord's name in vain using it to make yourself look good? Can you think of a way you do this?

2. Talk about the huge difference between using God's name as a swear word and to build up your own authority and using it to call on the Lord in every trouble, in prayer, in praise, and to give thanks. Is the difference only in your words? Or is the difference in your heart? Read Mark 8:34 and talk about what it means to deny yourself to live a life of praise to God.

Vine > Branches = Truth

"Abide in Me, and I in you. As the branch cannot bear fruit by itself, unless it abides in the vine, neither can you, unless you abide in Me. I am the vine; you are the branches. Whoever abides in Me and I in him, he it is that bears much fruit, for apart from Me you can do nothing. . . . If you keep My commandments, you will abide in My love, just as I have kept My Father's commandments and abide in His love."

—Jesus in John 15:4–5, 10

BECOMING INDEPENDENT FROM YOUR PARENTS is a little like a root canal. The extraction is necessary, painful, and complicated, and the process leaves you emotionally bleeding and with a hole for years to come. If you can still remember some of the stupid stuff you did during those angst-filled years, your emotional bleeding might last a long time.

I still cringe about the way I behaved in my early twenties, when I was struggling with God and the reverence my parents had for Him. During my years of rebelling, I worked with my dear friend Amy at a Christian camp in California. Her dad had been a pastor, and my family had been the kind who went to church several times a week. We both grew up in houses where the Lord's name was A Very Big Deal.

Although we grew up thousands of miles away from each other, we were kindred souls. Both of us had inherited our parents' faith traditions, and now we were trying to figure out which parts we wanted to keep.

Actually, I can't speak for Amy, but that's what the summer felt like to me. I was asking hard questions: What good was God in my life? What if I didn't pray? What if I skipped church and all the Bible studies? What if I cursed and cussed and wore T-shirts that said "Jesus Is My Homeboy"?

I think I wanted to offend God. Or more accurately, I wanted Him to know the new terms of our relationship. I charged into the next chapter of my life with Him as a secondary character, an unimportant extra. Amy was going through the same rebelliousness. When we stole the Communion wine and when we got drunk in Irish pubs in San Francisco, we did it with the swagger of the newly independent rebels we were.

After camp, and for the next decade, Amy and I stayed in close touch through emails and vacations together. When Catie was two and I was hugely pregnant with the twins, Amy flew to Houston to make meals for our family. I hadn't seen her since her wedding, and we both had lived some bumpy life. Amy had become a stepmom, and her husband, Nick, had been deployed to Iraq for fourteen months. Now Nick was back from serving as a military police officer, and Amy was scared that his scars were deeper than they first seemed. When we talked, we had lost some of our rebels' swagger; fear hummed just below our words.

This is when my conversations with Amy began to change. We started talking about God more. I think this is because we were both realizing—in a deep way—that we weren't indestructible or independent. I didn't want full custody of my life anymore. I needed God.

Then, for both of us, our thirties were full of more hard lessons—infertility and chronic illness for me and career changes and Nick's PTSD for Amy. More and more, we were getting involved in our churches and crying out to God for help. We were realizing how little we really controlled and how much we needed Him.

By the time we turned forty, Nick had admitted that his martini-a-night habit had gotten out of control and that he was an alcoholic. He checked himself into a rehab center. Amy and Nick were in the fight of their lives. Addiction felt bigger than either one of them. They needed God to change Nick's story.

And He did.

Through AA, God showed Nick how much He loved and forgave him and the ways He still wanted to use his life. Nick's pastor asked him to talk to other veterans who were struggling with PTSD. Nick couldn't tell the story of what God had done in his life without tears. When Amy emailed me a copy of his testimony, I cried too. This was the God our parents trusted and taught us to love. This God deserved every bit of our praise. Separately, across the country from each other, Amy and I had both come full circle to our parents' faith.

Just like a real root canal, the process of independence was painful, but it seemed like that's what I needed to do before I could mature. It isn't true for everyone of course, but for me, pushing God away showed me what was missing from that kind of life—Him.

Now I know that declaring independence from God makes about as much sense as a leaf declaring independence from its tree. That leaf's declaration is also its suicide note.

Amy and I aren't the only ones with emotional bleeding in our stories. Lots of us push God away before we learn firsthand who He is and why He is worthy of worship. We make jokes that use His name in vain. It's funny to take something so sacred and make it a punch line. Underlying the joke is always this question: What's the big deal about God, anyway?

I want every one of us to *get* what the big deal is. And so does God.

I want us to realize that this is the place we need to be, the place of truly understanding our dependence on God. This place, this sweet spot of needing a Savior, is the beginning of our story with Him, the start of the Holy Spirit changing our lives.

YOUR STORY/GOD'S STORY

1. Tell the story of defining your faith as your own. Did you try for independence from your family? from God? What did you discover?

2. When God seems silent, we might decide He doesn't care about us. We want His attention! Where is He? Talk about when this happens. Has your pride ever clouded your vision to see the work God is doing in your life? What can change your vision?

3. Read John 10:25–28. Jesus tells the Pharisees about His identity and that of His followers. What does this tell us about what followers of Christ look like? What promise does He make in verse 28?

4. God defines Himself. He is kindness (Romans 11:22). He is gracious (Exodus 34:5–6). He is holy (Isaiah 6:3). He is love (1 John 4:16). He is all powerful (Matthew 19:26), He is everywhere at once (Psalm 139), and He knows everything (Romans 16:27). Where do you see these qualities of God in your life?

5. How does understanding this commandment change the way you see your relationship with God? Are you using His name to curse, swear, or lie? How can you change the way you talk about God?

PRAY . . .

Lord, You are powerful and perfect. Even when I run from You, You never stop pursuing me. Help me know Your love and trust that it never fails, Lord. Help me to see Jesus as Your gift of that love. In His redeeming name. Amen.

Microwaving the Sacred

For by the grace given to me I say to everyone among you not to think of himself more highly than he ought to think, but to think with sober judgment, each according to the measure of faith that God has assigned.

—Paul in Romans 12:3

So, I THINK IT'S SAFE TO ADMIT that we all secretly believe our way is the best way. This is what it means to be human, isn't it? If the world just did things our way, there would be a lot less pain/fights/stupid people/sin/bad drivers/ fill in the blank.

Perhaps this smugness happens most in our ideas about God. Our relationship with Him is both personal and universal. What I mean is that each of us has an intimate, close-up relationship with God—and so does everyone else.

More on our opinions about God in a minute. First, let's talk about the other place where everyone believes their tastes are exactly right. Food. God and food. Beliefs about the right way to worship God and how food should taste have probably started more fights than anything else.

My friend Chandra learned about the fights food can start over several Thanksgivings. She had strong opinions about how that day should be celebrated. And so did her mother-in-law.

Chandra's husband, Charlie, was raised by a real Southern cook. His mom's name is Edna, and there's nothing she loves more than putting together a huge formal meal. The spread at their house is legendary: two turkeys (one fried and one brined and roasted), sausage–corn bread dressing, bacon-and-green-bean casserole, buttery mashed potatoes, and many pies and cakes. There is so much food, they need two banquet tables.

After Chandra and Charlie were married, Edna recruited Chandra to her Thanksgiving vision. Chandra thought Edna's whole production was funny. Her own family did a small-scale, simple Thanksgiving, and she couldn't imagine someone caring so much about gravy flavors.

By Chandra's third year in the family, Edna's Thanksgiving had started to bug her on a deeper level. Why should sweet Edna exhaust herself for such a feast? It was a waste of energy.

The next year, Chandra offered to host the meal at her house and take care of the turkeys and dressing. Edna asked to help dozens of times, but Chandra refused her. Then she ordered two smoked turkeys from a mail-order meat company and bought pans of ready-made dressing from a nice restaurant in town. Edna ate the ready-made turkeys and dressing without saying much.

The next year, Chandra really wanted to show Edna just how casual Thanksgiving could be. She ordered every dish—from the turkey to the pecan pies—from the grocery store, and she microwaved it all a few minutes before the family arrived. Although some people mentioned missing the old family recipes, no one said much else about the food. It just wasn't a big deal.

But Chandra was worried. Edna had been silent. Before the family gathered for Christmas, Chandra called Edna to see what she had thought about Thanksgiving. Wasn't she relieved to not have to do all that fuss?

But no. Edna explained that she *loved* the fuss of a big family gathering. She believed a holiday meal absolutely meant homemade stuffing, linen napkins, and champagne flutes.

Here's what Chandra learned when she paid closer attention to the work of Edna's Thanksgiving: all that shopping, stirring, marinating, and fussing built anticipation for the holiday. When she stopped by her mother-in-law's house a few days before the feast and Edna was baking corn bread, the whole house smelled fantastic.

As I've been thinking about the Second Commandment and why God cares how we treat His name, I've thought about Chandra and what she learned about china versus Chinet. What did she lose when she tried to do Thanksgiving her way, with less preparation and formality? What is the point of ceremony in our lives, anyway?

Thanksgiving isn't just another Thursday lunch. Thanks to the big deal we make of the holiday, other beautiful parts take place. When we polish the silver candlesticks and brine the turkey for two days, we are celebrating something special. In this celebration, we find hidden blessings of tradition, family, fellowship, and more.

Do we also find hidden blessings when we give God's name and the Sabbath the ceremony they deserve? Do we better understand our proper relationship to our holy God when we dress up for church, kneel at the altar, and celebrate the Lord's Supper as Jesus' holy body and blood? You bet we do.

I guess you could argue that none of this high-church ceremony is necessary. God makes it clear that He's okay with come-as-you-are and two-or-three-gathered-in-His-name. And I totally get that God loves simple, genuine worship.

But here's what else I'm learning: Our prideful hearts quickly turn casual into unimportant, and simple into whatever-works-for-us. I'm seeing convenience-over-fanfare isn't always the best formula.

These little acts of obedience and awe for God change our view of Him. On our knees, we can see that God is a very big deal—and that this is the best news in the world.

We don't worship a simple, meek God. We worship the hugely impressive Master of the universe. He doesn't need our worship, but we *need* to worship. The ceremony, the set-apart, and the holy remind us that God is all powerful and His love is all consuming.

He wants us to experience the full, blinding, unbelievable power of His passion for us. He wants us to experience the truth that He is worthy of ceremony and worthy of our worship.

YOUR STORY/GOD'S STORY

1. Talk about your history of microwaving the sacred. When have you reduced God's name to what's convenient for you?

2. Here's why most of us stop giving God's name any ceremony: He doesn't seem like that big of a deal. In fact, our own thoughts and opinions seem way more important. When your faith is detached, praising God's name seems as natural as putting on your wedding dress for din-

ner at McDonalds. Read Lamentations 3:22–24 and Romans 5:5. What does it mean that God's mercies are new every morning? Do you believe that right now? If not, what can reignite your faith?

3. What's lost when we microwave the sacred? When your worship is casual all the time, what happens to the way you view your Savior? Where do you see that happening in your church or your community?

4. Read Luke 1:46–55, Mary's song of praise. When Mary gets the biggest news in the history of the world, she praises God and says He is holy and doing great things for her. Talk about how this moment perfectly shows a dressed-up-Thanksgiving-dinner-ceremonial moment of God's name. Have you ever had a moment like this?

5. Think about how you use God's name now, and how you could use it more in praise and to give thanks.

PRAY . . .

Lord, Your name is worth ceremony and celebration, but my pride tells me it's not. Help me to understand how powerful You are and how much You love me. Help me to give Jesus' name the weight and worship it deserves. In His redeeming name. Amen.

Real Sunshine & the
Chick-fil-A Drive-Through

For at one time you were darkness, but now you are light in the Lord.
Walk as children of light (for the fruit of light is found in all that is good
and right and true), and try to discern what is pleasing to the Lord.

—Paul in Ephesians 5:8–10

DAYS I'M FEELING TIRED AND OVERWHELMED are not great days to visit the Chick-fil-A drive-through. I know this, but the cold, sweet cookies-and-cream milkshake calls to me. The sugar rush seems like the perfect pick-me-up on days when life has taken off a layer of my skin. Also, the kids love their nuggets, so I can grab dinner at the same time.

The problem is that everyone seems to feel this way about Chick-fil-A. The drive-through line is always crowded with other people who are trying to heal their grouchiness with milkshakes and nuggets. Everyone is revving their engines to get their fried chicken and ice cream and get out of there.

Last week, on an afternoon just like this, I mindlessly inched in front of another car. The other driver rolled down her window and started yelling at me about cutting her off. "Look, %$&*!" she called. "You are not #$@#ing next!"

I stared at her. And then I started crying. Because, of course, I was already in the yucky mind-set of thinking an ice cream shake would cheer me up. Clearly I couldn't handle yelling and cussing.

She shook her head and vroomed in front of me. There was a Christian fish on the back of her Suburban. Also, as she drove past, I saw through her window that the rhinestones on her black T-shirt spelled out "Blessed."

The kids were fascinated; I was angry. After dinner, I told Mike what bugged me the most. Wasn't it crazy that this woman, who was so hateful and mean, was advertising herself as a Christian?

"Maybe she's just an angry person," he said. "Or maybe she was having a bad day. Or maybe she's just disappointed."

"Disappointed in what?"

"I don't know. Disappointed in life. Maybe she feels like we all feel sometimes, like she's kind of failing at everything important."

Okay, probably so. After all, that's the way I was feeling, and the reason I was at Chick-fil-A in the first place. My day had been full of broken promises, broken dishes, and a deep brokenness inside me. Maybe hers had been too. Maybe the crowded Chick-fil-A line was *it* for her.

We both needed more love, more peace, more grace. Maybe that explained her Christian fish and "Blessed" shirt. She was searching for some healing.

Actually, aren't we all looking for this kind of healing? We know we're jaundiced, and we set out looking for medicinal vitamin D. This leads us to Christian culture. The Christian culture's ideas about Christ seem to be exactly what we need. Wear a cross necklace, join church groups, advertise that you belong to Jesus, and call yourself blessed. Done. Totally fulfilled.

Except not really.

What I'm starting to learn is that Christian culture is just the tanning bed. Under this artificial, human-created light, we can still act however we want. Anyone can be Christian if we're the ones setting the rules. Turn down the heat when it gets too hot, and pull out any body parts you don't want in the light.

For real encounters with God, He invites us into His bright, brilliant sunshine. This can be so hard. Sitting in that white-hot moment of confession is so, so awful. Finally admitting "I keep getting this wrong, God. And I need Your help" is incredibly painful in the moment.

But God always gives us what we need next. He gives us real forgiveness, love, and grace. Suddenly the sunshine isn't burning-hot uncomfortable. It's warm. Medicinal. Comforting.

When we cling only to the *idea* of Christ, we are sick people offering a sick culture a Jesus we have re-created to be something He's not. We've taken His potent, powerful work on the cross and watered it down to an impotent symbol.

More and more I realize it's not the Christian tanning-bed life I want. I don't need fake faith, where everything is designed to make me look good. This kind of vain Christianity offers no real healing.

What would the world look like if all of us who claimed to follow Jesus, who attached His name to our lives, tried to live like He tells us to? What if we believed calling ourselves Christian meant sacrifice and repentance? What if we showed the world that calling ourselves Christian meant allowing our hearts to be changed? What if we had such awe for His name, for crosses and symbols of Him, that we didn't claim them so lightly?

Could we listen more to the voice of the Holy Spirit? Could we input more of God's Word in our lives and output less about what good Christians we are?

You and I are ready for this up-close life with Christ. God tells us we are ready to stop merely calling ourselves Christians. We are ready for true healing through Christ and His Word and Sacraments.

We are ready for the Holy Spirit to open our eyes to God's bright and brilliant love.

YOUR STORY/GOD'S STORY

1. Does it ever feel like the Christian culture is so much louder in this world than Christ is? Talk about how we cling to the symbols of Christianity. Have you ever gone through a season when you tried to find real healing from Christian culture rather than from Christ? Tell your story.

2. Read Matthew 23:27–28. The Pharisees loved religious culture, but they couldn't recognize the Savior. Can you think of an example of how we do this today? Why does Jesus warn us against lives that lack real transformation?

3. As the saying goes, "There's no such thing as bad press." How do you

think this applies to the Christian culture? Could it be that lots of people wearing "Blessed" T-shirts and cross necklaces gets the message of God's love out there, even if it is a little watered down? Read Matthew 15:8; Isaiah 29:13; and 1 John 2:9. Is this getting God's name into the world or using it in vain?

4. Read Psalm 51:10 and Ezekiel 36:26. Real transformation means God trades our dirty, stony hearts for clean hearts of flesh. What does this look like in your life? Do we have any say in whether we want a new heart, one flooded with God's healing, brilliant love?

5. Luther says not to deceive or lie by God's name. When we call ourselves Christians but don't live lives that show His love, we deceive by His name. In what ways do you need God to change your life so you show the world His love and power?

PRAY . . .

Powerful Lord, You are the bright, brilliant light of my life. Help me to refuse fake, weak versions of You. Show me Your love in new ways, Lord. Lead me to a deeper relationship through Your Son, Jesus. In His redeeming name. Amen.

Our Father, Who Trademarked His Name

"Pray then like this: 'Our Father in heaven, hallowed be Your name.'"

—Jesus in Matthew 6:9

PERHAPS THE MOST SACRED WAY we use God's name is when we pray. Praising God in worship is also sacred, but prayer often feels personal—and desperate. Calling on the Creator of the universe and then asking Him to change your most desperate situations is so humbling that it's mind-boggling.

Throughout my life, my Aunt Katie has shown me what powerful, intimate prayer looks like in action. She introduced me to what a gift prayer is, and that has changed my kids and me.

Aunt Katie has been my mom's friend—and prayer partner—for almost five decades. She's not really my aunt, but this is the title we use to kind of capture who she is in my life and the life of our family.

Years ago, through Moms in Prayer, Aunt Katie discovered that praying was the only match for her fear. She became a Stephen Minister at her church. She volunteered forty hours a week at a ministry that offers prayer for anyone in Houston. She prayed for her sons when they failed out of school. She prayed for her husband's career, for the pastors at their church, and for those who don't know Jesus. Aunt Katie prays like she breathes: in and out, and all the time.

Aunt Katie has prayed for our family for years. She prayed for us to have a baby. She prayed when I miscarried. When our twins were high-risk babies, she gathered prayer warriors from all over our city to pray for them.

Mike and I pray, but we're not quite where Aunt Katie is. If life is made up of frequencies, then we're often riding the Fear Frequency. The pulsating engine driving our days is terror that we won't accomplish enough, terror that everything we love will be taken from us, terror that we are bad parents. This is probably not just our family; it may be yours too. Our minds are little fear factories—downloading life's events and uploading scary scenarios of the worst possible outcomes.

But prayer has changed this for us. Aunt Katie starts her prayers by calling on Jesus, who is holy and perfect and powerful. And right there—already—the problem moves from our own scared minds to the realm of Someone Who Can Do Something About This. This is a miracle. Seriously. I've seen it happen six hundred times. Prayer. The name of Jesus. Talking to our holy, powerful Father changes us. Our shoulders relax and our breath deepens.

When Aunt Katie asks our kids "Can we talk to Jesus about this?" and she starts a prayer in His name, the whole frequency of our household changes. Suddenly we're not running on the Fear Frequency; we're in calm and confident territory. God takes us out of terror-tory and into His realm.

Maybe this is why Jesus taught us to begin the Lord's Prayer with His name. This reminds our scared hearts that He is sacred. God doesn't need for us to tell Him He is holy, but *we* need it. We need to be reminded, several times and with every prayer, that we are now talking to the one who can change the situation of our lost job or our lost shoes. Prayer to anyone other than our triune God is just a bunch of words.

When our kids ask why we can't say the Lord's name in vain and why we can't use OMG, we talk about prayer. We talk about the comfort that comes from calling on Jesus' name and knowing He is holy. We talk about what Aunt Katie has taught us about prayer. We talk about what would be lost if we abused His name. This wouldn't change who God is, but it would dilute the way we see Him, and it would break His commandment to us.

Our kids understand this. Thanks to Aunt Katie and the thousands of prayers she's started with "Dear Jesus," with "O Lord," and with "Our Father," our kids know His name is sacred.

Thanks to prayer in Jesus' name, our kids understand they are loved by the most sacred, holy, powerful, gracious Power in the universe, and He hears every one of their prayers.

YOUR STORY/GOD'S STORY

1. Every person's prayer life is different. Talk about yours. Do you pray memorized prayers? before bed? constantly throughout the day? when you're scared? Look at Mark 11:24 and John 14:13–14. What's your testimony about prayer in your own life?

2. Talk about how calling on God's name reminds you who He is. What about using His name in vain? Does this dilute your understanding of His power?

3. Read John 15:16. See how Jesus presents prayer here. Why do you think He explains our identity as chosen first? How does this clarify our relationship with God? How does understanding this change your prayer?

4. If you started a Mexican restaurant, made your branding a green mermaid, and called yourself Starbucks, the coffee chain would sue you for copyright infringement. They already own the name Starbucks, and you can't borrow their popularity because that would confuse people who go to your restaurant looking for pumpkin spice lattes. In the same way, God has trademarked His name for us to use in the ways He wants us to use it—in prayer and in praise. This means we can't use His name in whatever ways we want. Why is this concept important to your prayer life?

5. The explanation of this commandment says we should call upon God's name in every trouble. Yes! Exactly this! How would doing this look in your life? What troubles are you facing or will you face this week? Could you interject more prayer into your life?

PRAY . . .

Father, hallowed be Thy name. When I say Your name, help me to understand Your love and power. Help me not weaken Your name by using it in vain. Thank You for sending Jesus, who intercedes for me. In His redeeming name. Amen.

Honor the Sabbath

"Remember the Sabbath day, to keep it holy. Six days you shall labor, and do all your work, but the seventh day is a Sabbath to the LORD your God. On it you shall not do any work, you, or your son, or your daughter, your male servant, or your female servant, or your livestock, or the sojourner who is within your gates. For in six days the LORD made heaven and earth, the sea, and all that it is in them, and rested on the seventh day. Therefore the LORD blessed the Sabbath day and made it holy."

–God in Exodus 20:8—11

[Jesus] said to them, "The Sabbath was made for man, not man for the Sabbath."

—Jesus in Mark 2:27

LAST SATURDAY NIGHT, my husband and I got a babysitter and headed to a new coffee shop, Tout Suite, in downtown Houston. It's a fantastic place to work. I don't mean it's fantastic for the baristas (although I'm sure it is since the coffee is delicious and, therefore, they're very popular). I mean it's a fantastic place for the rest of us to work.

Mike and I pulled out our laptops, put on our headphones, and joined the sixty or so others staring at their computer screens. They were high school and college students, other writers, and those whose work had spilled over into the weekend. We all sat side by side, clicking away our Saturday night, getting our work done.

Not to sound ungrateful for the reliable Wi-Fi and croissants as big as my head, but I wonder why we all have so much work to do. Mike and I gave up eating dinner with our kids, visiting a friend in the hospital, seeing a band we love, inviting over friends, and looking each other in the eye and talking. Why? So we could accomplish more. What is driving this need to work all day, every day of the week?

I'm not sure, but I know what's *not* driving our need to accomplish more—all the things that are really important in life. Here are a few: the transudation that comes with listening to truly good music, the need our bodies have for deep rest, and the joy that comes with gathering with our favorite people.

Considering the important hours we all give up to work, it would seem that we have no choice. It would seem that we have become slaves to a lifestyle of hard work every single hour of every single day.

Are we?

Thousands of years ago, God gave the Israelites (who were actual slaves) the Sabbath as a much-needed rest. A perfect present from Someone who loved them very much, the Sabbath was a nuanced, layered, essential rest for His people. The Sabbath was not only a day of rest from their slavery, but it was also a foreshadowing of what was to come. One day, they would live in the Promised Land, where they would not be slaves. One day, they would live in heaven and have eternal rest.

The fantastic news for you and me is that God gives us this same gift today. Receiving this gift is like inheriting your great-grandma's two-karat wedding ring—the one that is both ancient yet modern, and also really fun to wear. The Sabbath is a beautiful mixture of God's covenant with us from long ago, of really good guidance for us today, and of what we have to look forward to in heaven, thanks to our Savior.

The Sabbath was, is, and will be the holy day in our lives.

Let's stop working and enjoy it.

THOUGHTS ABOUT THIS COMMANDMENT

1. Martin Luther explains the Third Commandment this way: "We should fear and love God so that we do not despise preaching and His Word, but hold it sacred and gladly hear and learn it." We don't use the word *despise* so often today, but other words for this attitude could be *neglect* and *undervalue*. Take a few minutes to talk about where you're at with church. Do you neglect or undervalue gathering to hear God's Word?

2. You'll see in the women's stories for this commandment that we all endure different seasons: times we go through when we gladly hear and learn God's Word, and times when church and Bible study get buried by our busyness and cynicism. Tell your story of going through both seasons.

Holy Work

So those who received His word were baptized, and there were added that day about three thousand souls. And they devoted themselves to the apostles' teaching and the fellowship, to the breaking of bread and the prayers. And awe came upon every soul, and many wonders and signs were being done through the apostles.

—the evangelist Luke in Acts 2:41–43

WHEN WE TALK ABOUT CHURCH, we usually assume we all mean the same experience, but church looks different to each of us. I don't just mean the ways different denominations celebrate, and I don't mean pipe organ versus electric guitar. I mean what we get out of church. You've probably had seasons when you show up like a brittle sponge, ready to soak up the goodness of friends, your favorite worship music, and poignant sermons filled with God's love for you.

You've also probably had times when you drag yourself to church, bitter and blind to anything good happening there at all.

This is a story about that second kind of season.

It started with our twins' Baptism, which goes down in our family history as one of our most stressful events. The anxiety was thanks to me acting like a control freak, the unpredictability of two infants, an attention-deprived toddler, and several out-of-town guests, all gathered for one long church service.

I started with good intentions, but the Baptism quickly moved from Sunday sacrament to wedding-level planning. What should the twins wear? Which godparent would hold which baby? Which Bible verses on which banner? And what about the pictures? Should the rest of us be in bright colors or white? What were appropriate favors for a Baptism party? Was it weird or festive for the babies to wear socks with crosses embroidered on them?

The night before, when I realized Sam didn't have a white swaddling blanket, I just about lost my mind. Everyone would be cringing at his ratty blue blanket, and the pictures would look ridiculous. At nine o'clock that night, I sent my bleary-eyed husband to Target for a Baptism-appropriate blanket.

I ask you, what *is* a Baptism-appropriate blanket?

Looking back, I can see that this crazy, hyper-controlled event started a season of what church looked like for us. Our kids were very small, and church became a stressful hour of keeping babies and toddlers shushed.

On Sunday morning, we packed their industrial-size diaper bags with enough pacifiers and coloring books to keep everyone quiet for the hour. Still, we could never make it through a service without one of the kids crying. More than once, Mike and I stood in the narthex together, me trying to discreetly breastfeed in a church dress while he reprimanded Catie for flying paper airplanes.

I started to dislike Sunday mornings. Church meant having to fix everyone's hair, wear special clothes, stand and sit, and follow so many rules. At this point in my life, I wasn't showering regularly, drinking coffee or wine (thanks, breastfeeding), or sleeping through the night. I fantasized about freedom, about locking myself in my closet and reading *People* while eating handfuls of cookie dough. Church was pretty much the opposite of all that.

One Sunday, the kids were sick and we missed. Sleeping in and not having to wrestle kids into Sunday outfits and car seats was so nice. The next Sunday, another kid had a cough, and we missed again. I felt guilty about not being at church—but not that guilty. We missed the next week too, just because we couldn't get out the door in time. We were so late we decided to just go out for donuts.

The next week, it was six thousand times harder to get to church. And when we got there, it was a Baptism Sunday for another family, which meant the service would be very, very long.

This family with the baby getting baptized had several other kids, but theirs were teenagers, and this last baby had been a surprise. The baby didn't have five godparents or seven pews of family members in attendance. Instead, just the immediate family gathered around the font. They were in jeans and tennis shoes. The baby was wearing a (blue!) onesie.

As the pastor poured the water over the infant's head, the mom started to cry. She watched this holy moment with such transcendence on her face. It's the look people sometimes get when taking Communion.

For the first time since the twins were baptized, I saw that sacrament for what it was. Not what the baby was wearing, not if the shoes of the siblings were tied, not whether the mom had lost the baby weight. In that moment, I remembered something bigger was happening at church than what was going on in my tiny pew.

More than that, I felt incredibly aware of that other mom's spiritual vulnerability. It was clear by her face, by her priorities, by her tears that her heart was soft, fertile ground for the seed of faith. She was able to see the miracle of God claiming His child.

How different had church been for her these past few months? Had she understood that worship is so much more than what the kids are wearing, more than rules about when to sit and stand, more than a chore? How had God's Word changed her during these church services—while I was checking my watch, hoping we would make pancakes at McDonalds?

When had I become such a cynic, so controlling and self-absorbed? When had my view of God and church shrunk? I felt like the kid who misses the shooting star because she's fiddling with her flashlight. God was so much bigger than my limitations. I was tired and stressed out; *God* wasn't.

Part of taking a Sabbath is realizing the experience probably will do very little for your pride. For those of us who find our value in checking things off our to-do lists, the act of quiet worship may seem like a waste of time.

But God wants us to realize why this is not true. He knows that the other parts of us—the parts that are not pride, conceit, and ego—need worship desperately. This is the reason He tells us to rest and worship.

That tender, vulnerable part of you, the part where the Holy Spirit is working, is so ready to hear the faith-fortifying words in the sermon, to pray and sing praise songs with hundreds of others, and to see God's holy work.

Slowly, God is teaching me about worship. He's teaching me that no one came to the twins' Baptism for good cake or to make sure we were a picture-perfect family. He's helping me learn that faith, vulnerability, joy, and worship are all a tight knot.

At the center of that knot is the God who loved us enough to send His Son. This loving Father does not want us to miss His care, His holiness, His love, and His sacred work.

YOUR STORY/GOD'S STORY

1. Tell the story about what church looks like to you. Do you find worship fills you up and refreshes you? Or are you in a cynical season? If so, what do you think is at the root of this? How can it change?

2. Read Hebrews 10:25. Why do believers stop meeting together for worship? Every year, fewer Christians attend church. What's the cause behind this decline? Is this a new problem?

3. Read Matthew 18:20. What is the fantastic news here for us? Worship is not only us worshiping Jesus, it's also Jesus doing what? What does this mean for you when planning your week?

4. Read Psalm 26:8. Talk about the different parts of the church service and what blessings God gives us there. Do you have a story about which of these are especially meaningful to you?

5. What do you need to do differently to gladly hear God's Word and learn from it? Pray that God works in your heart so that you delight in His merciful love through reading His Word and in worship.

PRAY . . .

Lord, You deserve all my worship and praise. So often, church seems like a burden. Change my heart so that I better understand how much my soul needs to hear Your Word. Help me to celebrate my Savior and the gift of His sacrifice. In His redeeming name. Amen.

Praise & Popularity

For God alone, O my soul, wait in silence, my hope is from Him.

—David in Psalm 62:5

AFTER BOB DYLAN BECAME A CHRISTIAN, he wrote the song "Gotta Serve Somebody" about Romans 6 and the idea that, like it or not, we are all in constant service to someone. Maybe we serve ourselves or popular opinion or friends or God. But the way we fill our hours every week reveals whom we serve.

As women, we often find ourselves serving others; lots of times this is to fulfill our own need to be liked. This is what happened to me after eight years of staying at home with our kids. Our baby started preschool, and I suddenly had full days to shower, go places, and make some friends.

I quickly discovered the key to making friends is to say yes. Say yes to room mothering, yes to PTL, yes to helping with the church carnival, and yes to starting a school newspaper. Very quickly, I found my new identity: Yes Girl.

The more people I agreed to help, the more my phone vibrated with texts from new friends. People loved that I helped plan class parties and galas. Long meetings turned into lunches and then into invitations to dinners. Dinners turned into more friends, more appreciation, more yeses.

This cycle churned through the school year. Although I didn't fully realize it at the time, my life was becoming a weird economy of trading my time for compliments and friends. I would do the tedious volunteer work, as long as the world agreed I was useful.

Until April, when I got a cold I couldn't shake, and I slipped into a funk. My calendar was full, my in-box was full, and my voicemail was full, but I felt empty. Every day looked like the day before it. One Sunday morning before sunrise, I found myself standing over the sink, eating last night's enchiladas, wishing I could go back to bed and skip the full day of church, practices, parties, and obligations.

The weight of everyone's needs was too heavy, and I had nothing left to give. I had no plans to answer emails, no desire to solve anyone's problem, and no energy to get the kids ready for church. The only activity I could muster that Sunday was crawling back into bed and pulling the covers over my head. Mike got the kids dressed, and they went to church without me.

The next morning, while walking the twins into kindergarten, I saw my friend Melissa. We hadn't been friends long, but I had noticed she didn't volunteer much.

She asked me about the class Easter party, but I answered by saying I was worn out. Too worn out, certainly, to know the party details. Somehow, I thought she might have some wisdom about this empty feeling.

She did. She told me she had gone through a similar breakdown. She talked about how she's a reformed approval addict. Now she pays more attention to how she uses her time. She's trying to live as a soul that needs nourishing instead of just playing roles that will make people like her. She told me about finding her identity in her relationship with the Lord rather than whom she could make happy.

Everything she was saying brought the past school year into brilliant focus. Yes. My identity was firmly rooted in whether or not people liked me. I wanted to cry from the embarrassment of that.

As the next couple of months passed, I paid attention to where I found my identity. Why did I need all these people relying on me? Why was I expecting them to supply my identity for me? Looking to them for my value placed a huge burden on these people. They may have been struggling with their own value; they certainly didn't have the time or energy to tell me I was valuable. That wasn't their job in the first place.

That is God's job.

I started to see that, yes, my spiritual needs were in a fight against the roles I was playing. When I fed the roles, they seemed to win: I was hungry for more affirmations, desperate to make more friends, agitated when I tried to relax. But when I went to church, rested, and read God's Word, my soul won. And I wanted more of all of these.

I prayed and asked the Holy Spirit to help me clear out some quiet time in my life. Slowly, intentionally, and painfully, I reclaimed my life as one soul following God.

Let me tell you, saying yes is so much more fun than saying no. Taking on everyone else's burdens is like a drug; giving them back is rehab. My not being everything to everyone meant saying good-bye to all these friends, and I almost couldn't do it. But I knew that I had to. It took a little breakdown for me to take a break. God had my attention. I was ready for His change.

Rest and spiritual care were the refreshment my tired body and thirsty spirit needed. Filled up with the Holy Spirit, I could see the quiet ways He was moving in my life.

This was a Sabbath.

YOUR STORY/GOD'S STORY

1. Have you ever (during finals in college, during a busy time at work, or during an especially exhausting season of motherhood) had a breakdown? What was going on that kept you from rest? Were you finding your value in a person or place besides God?

2. How is observing a Sabbath part of caring for your soul? How does time with God help root your identity as His follower? How does worshiping God stop you from believing you are your own god or anyone else's?

3. Read Romans 6:6. Think about your identity and whom you serve. Talk about what life looks like when we live to please others or ourselves. What about when we live to please God?

4. Look at Hebrews 4:9–11. Here God talks about the most important rest we will experience as believers. What kind of eternal rest does He promise us?

5. When you find your identity in who others say you are, you devalue your identity as God's child. Pray for God to change your heart so you crave personal encounters with Christ through God's Word. What would it look like for church and Scripture to be sacred in your life?

Lord, You pull me back to You, even when I wander to find my value in what the world says is important. Help me to see that my forever identity is as Your daughter. Transform my heart so I want to live in that identity and do Your will. Thank You for Jesus, whose sacrifice means I'm Your forgiven child. In His redeeming name. Amen.

The Rhythm of
Kale Chips & French Fries

"Six days shall work be done, but on the seventh day is a Sabbath of solemn rest, a holy convocation. You shall do no work. It is a Sabbath to the LORD *in all your dwelling places."*

—God in Leviticus 23:3

GROWING UP IN THE '70S AND '80S, we ate a lot of processed, deliciously junky foods. Frozen waffles for breakfast, bologna sandwiches on soft white bread at lunch, and ready-made lasagna for dinner.

When I became a mom, I fed my kids these same foods. Except Mike has a sweet tooth, so we also ate lots of chocolate pudding cups and Twizzlers.

A couple of years ago, I had to admit that eating all this junk wasn't working for my body. My friend Connie is a nurse practitioner, and she preaches how important the digestive tract is to overall health. I didn't want to believe it, but that processed food and sugar was making me sluggish and irritable.

For the next few months, I ate differently. Less sugar, less dairy, less gluten, less salt. No fast food, no wine, no lasagna, no nightly bowl of cereal.

By the time summer came, I was feeling so much better. My energy was back, I fell asleep quickly at night, my skin glowed. These months of fasting from my favorite foods were exactly what my body had needed. I stopped craving French fries and started telling everyone how tasty green smoothies are.

Then our family shifted into our summer routine, and I was ready to taste my favorite foods again. Slowly, we slipped into our old eating habits. We took long road trips and ate French fries, cheese curds, and lots of thick frozen custard. Whole days at the beach ended with stops for waffle cones dripping with peanut butter ice cream. We had lazy family nights, pausing Uno only long enough to order pizza. Popsicles every day, and Frappucinos every time we drove home from swim practice. Six months later, I was sluggish again.

I confessed to Connie that I had fallen off the green-smoothie wagon. I wanted to eat vegetables for lunch, but not every lunch for the rest of my life. Eventually I needed cupcakes and pizza. I was one of those people who couldn't stay committed to the food my body needed.

Connie pointed out that I wasn't failing as badly as I thought. We talked about how my months of healthy eating were still helping me today. Even as I was getting out of control with the junk food, I had already learned how to feed my body. At any time, I could go back to eating clean for a bit. I had learned how to cook chicken soup and broccoli that my family loved. More important, I knew how good we all felt when we ate vegetables more often than mac and cheese.

And yes, seasons of kale chips made us appreciate the French-fry seasons more. Weeks of steel-cut oatmeal made the Pop-Tarts that much more delicious.

Our bodies work best with a rhythm of feasting on foods we love and then fasting from those to eat foods we need. Peas and grilled chicken most days, but also brownie-bottomed pecan pie after Sunday lunch.

Connie talked about how the digestive system can handle only so much trans fat and soy lecithin before it needs a break. Just like the body can handle only so much work before it needs a break. Just like the farmland needs a rest from crops, just like kids need a vacation from school, just like we need exercise after a Netflix binge.

Why, then, is it so hard to admit that our bodies need a break from work? I can see the toll that stress takes on me. My days are filled with fights with my husband, guilt that my kid is struggling in school, frustration that I can't accomplish more, and fear about the violence right here in my own city. After so, so many days of my soul absorbing this sin, it's sluggish. I need God's cleanse.

Did God engineer me like this so I would keep coming back to Him for forgiveness, peace, and faith? When Jesus said "The Sabbath was created for man, not man for the Sabbath," was He talking about how desperately we need this different, holy day as part of our week's rhythm?

Yes. He was.

God is holy; He is set apart from this world. He is completely different from sinful anxiety. The pressure of this hard world will pollute your soul. A Sabbath is your invitation to rest and reconnect with God as He comes to you in the Divine Service. The rhythm of a day off, a fast from the to-do list, gives you a new perspective. You can go back into your week with a renewed faith and fresh security that come from knowing you belong to Him.

As we incorporate rest into our family's routine, I'm starting to see how important it is. The peace infiltrates our busy weeks. As time with God becomes our habit, we crave it more.

God is gradually showing us that some seasons of our lives are about more, about saying yes, and about doing.

And some seasons are about celebrating the rest He gives us in His Sabbath.

YOUR STORY/GOD'S STORY

1. What's your story of finding the rhythm of rest and work? Read Ecclesiastes 3:1–8, which is God's wisdom about the natural rhythm in our lives. Talk about your rhythms. When do you find yourself unable to take a break? What sin prompts this?

2. Life can become so busy, we translate "day of rest" into "day to finish the rest of the work." Read Genesis 2:3 and Exodus 20:8–11. The Sabbath is "the holy day." What does *holy* mean here?

3. In Leviticus 23:22, God tells His people an important spiritual truth: When you harvest your fields, don't collect everything; don't go all the way to the very edge. Instead, leave some for the poor. What about in your life? Do you harvest every bit of time and energy? Or do you practice "not gleaning to the edge of the field"? Also, what does God teach in Exodus 23:11? Why?

4. Chick-fil-A celebrates the Sabbath by giving their employees the day off to rest and worship. They recognize Sunday as different, as holy. Does this work as a business model? Why?

5. Luther's explanation of the commandment says we should not despise (or neglect) preaching and God's Word. Think about when this happens in your life. When you've used every bit of your energy and have not rested, is it easy for you to neglect God's Word? How can you better follow this commandment?

PRAY . . .

Lord, You show me the perfect example of work and rest, but the world teaches me a messed-up, unhealthy version. Recalibrate my relationship with work to fit Your rhythm. Help me to see You are my respite, Lord. Help me to rest in the promise of eternity with my Savior, Jesus. In His redeeming name. Amen.

Kicking & Screaming

"Come to Me, all who labor and are heavy laden, and I will give you rest. Take My yoke upon you, and learn from Me, for I am gentle and lowly in heart, and you will find rest for your souls. For My yoke is easy, and My burden is light."

—Jesus in Matthew 11:28–30

TAKING A SABBATH SOUNDS like a fabulous idea until you actually try it—kind of like riding your bike to work or agreeing to let your kid paint her own room.

Observing the Sabbath seems retro, noble, wise, and fun. But then you announce to everyone that your family will now begin observing the Sabbath, and right then, the effort to do this becomes complicated, legalistic, and very hard.

When our family tried to rest on the Sabbath, we discovered we were as terrible at this as we are at bedtime. Bedtime is my very least favorite part of the day because no one in our family can just let the day go. We must squeeze all productivity out of every single day. Everyone needs one more drink, one more story, one more kiss, one more question about what causes earthquakes. Most nights end with someone's tears as I walk down the steps, calling, "I AM DONE. JUST CLOSE YOUR EYES. EVERYTHING WILL SEEM BETTER IN THE MORNING."

When we tried to observe the Sabbath and rest, we discovered that relaxing is against our human drive to produce. Each of us was so used to the buzz of commitments and work, an empty Sunday seemed lazy. Mike and I are usually so plugged in to social networking, our switched-off cell phones felt lonely. We are so used to the pressure of a to-do list, the quiet together was strangely suffocating. We became restless, and we picked at each other.

After months of trying to get our family to rest on the Sabbath, I eventually gave up on the idea. No one complained when I let our Sundays fill back up with deadlines and work. We were going to be agitated and restless on Sunday afternoons anyway; we might as well get stuff done.

Then, last month, rest finally came. Our family woke up late for church, and the morning was a mad rush of scrunching hair into ponytails and eating muffins in the car. We were cranky and snapping at one another. "You forgot the offering check?" "That voters meeting is today?" And from the backseat, "All my clothes itch!"

Driving home from lunch and the meeting, we all dreaded the afternoon— loads of homework for the kids, deadlines for Mike and me, and we all needed to be at a birthday party at four o'clock.

Then we got stuck in traffic. We stewed in the highway parking lot in silence. The car was hot, and the mood was sour. Even the kids were too grouchy to bicker.

But soon, the silence felt different. I turned around to see all four kids asleep. They struggle to sleep in their beds, but they had conked out in their uncomfortable car seats, wearing itchy church clothes. When we pulled into the garage and Mike turned off the car, I surrendered to the heaviness of my fatigue, closed my eyes, and leaned my seat back. I heard Mike do the same.

An hour later, we all woke up, still in the car. We weren't grumpy or sweaty or mad that we had slept, but we were refreshed. I don't know what made us finally give in to rest, but that bit of sleep was exactly what we needed.

For each of us, that nap was a surrender to the Sabbath. It was like a little experiment: Could we close our eyes? If we weren't up and monitoring everything, what would fall apart?

The answer, of course, was nothing fell apart. We could rest. Our world didn't unravel. We were all fine. Better, actually.

As our family got ready for bed that night, we talked about naps. We talked about the story of Jesus and the thunderstorm. The disciples were freaking out about the storm that was swirling around them, and Jesus took a nap. Chaos everywhere, and Jesus, the only one who could do something about the storm, rested in the boat. He was peaceful.

When the disciples woke Jesus up, He reprimanded them, connecting their inability to relax to their lack of faith. His calming of that crazy storm had impressed the disciples. In that moment, they learned a little bit more about who Jesus was. He had everything under control, including the weather and any other terrifying chaos they could imagine.

Our kids loved this story. They loved imagining Jesus taking a nap. They loved the comfort of hearing that God rules all. They loved hearing that Jesus wasn't high strung or neurotic, but He was peaceful and confident. They loved knowing they could take a nap, totally relaxed by the idea God was taking care of them.

What about you? Is trusting that God can do anything the melatonin you need to rest? Could believing He loves you be anesthesia for your restless soul? Could you fall asleep thanking Him for true rest rather than cramming items onto your mental to-do list?

With the Sabbath, God is telling you to go ahead and take a nap. You are not in charge of the chaos of this world. You have no control over it, and the Holy Spirit wants to show you that Jesus takes perfect care of you.

Refreshed and rooted in this faith, you can better see ways to serve Him, you can better see ways to experience His love.

Even when you surrender to rest.

Especially when you do.

YOUR STORY/GOD'S STORY

1. Do you observe the Sabbath? If so, tell your story about what works and what doesn't. Where does God show you His grace in this commandment?

2. Work is an important part of our life's rhythm. In Genesis 2:19, God gave Adam the job of taking care of the Garden of Eden and naming the animals, even before sin entered the world. So we can see work isn't sinful—but our relationship with it can be. What does a good relationship with work look like for you? Where does rest fit into this?

3. Remember the context of the Third Commandment: The Israelites had worked as slaves seven days a week, so the Sabbath was a gift for them. They hadn't earned the right to rest; the day was a blessing from God. According to Matthew 11:28–30; Romans 4:5; and Colossians 2:16–17, Jesus transforms the Law, so we can rest in Him. As modern-day Christians, how is our Sabbath still a gift from God?

4. Six reasons to go to church: It's what God commands. It's what Jesus did. Other adults teach your kids about God. Jesus comes to us through the Sacraments and preaching of the Word. Going to church gives you the chance to encourage other believers. Praising and praying with other believers inspires your faith. In your life right now, which of these reasons resonates most with you?

5. Let's be glad for the Sabbath! Let's thank God for His gift of rest! Let's celebrate the Sabbath as the gift it is! Talk about habits you can change that will help you rest on the Sabbath. If you have a job that requires you to work weekends (in a health career, as a public servant, or a hospitality worker, for instance), how can you include worship and rest in your schedule?

PRAY . . .

Heavenly Father, absolutely everything in this world is under Your control. Wipe the pride from my eyes so I can see that. Show me Your power and love so I can understand it's okay to take a break. Thank You for Jesus, who was powerful enough to calm the storm and loving enough to die for my sins. In His redeeming name. Amen.

Honor Your Father & Mother

"Honor your father and your mother, that your days may be long in the land that the LORD your God is giving you."

—God in Exodus 20:12

When Jesus saw His mother and the disciple whom He loved standing nearby, He said to His mother, "Woman, behold, your son!" Then He said to the disciple, "Behold, your mother!" And from that hour the disciple took her to his own home.

—John, the disciple whom Jesus loved, in John 19:26–27

IF YOU LOVE MEMOIRS, YOU'RE IN TERRIFIC COMPANY. Every year, readers buy more and more of these tell-all stories about famous and not-so-famous people.

I think we read memoirs because we want to understand childhood. We want to crack the code of what the growing-up process should look like. What are the secrets here? What kinds of parents raise CEOs and comedians? What about those kids who grow up to be mass shooters? What mistakes did those parents make?

Actually, maybe we really read memoirs to ask different, harder questions: Was my childhood normal? Were my parents out of line? Am I messed up because of something they did?

These questions about our childhoods lead us to more questions. If my parents were horrible to me, can I ignore them now? Can I resent them for their mistakes? And if that feels good, can I also hold a grudge against my kids for not becoming what I want or need?

Many of us believe our folks were flawed. Looking back on our childhoods, it feels like our parents could have been both too needy and too aloof. Some can pinpoint seasons when their folks seemed more suited to raising golden retrievers than human children. Some can pinpoint seasons when their parents were not even suited for that.

This makes God's commandment to honor our parents seem like a tone-deaf ultimatum. Honor the people who held so much power in our most vulnerable seasons—and then didn't deliver?

Yes, God says in the Fourth Commandment. Honor them because family is *kabed* (weighty), in deep ways we can't understand. Honor them because this is a covenant relationship that lasts forever. Honor them to learn how to be an honorable mom. Most important, honor your parents to learn how to forgive them.

Forgiveness. This always seems to be what God is after with us, isn't it? No, He doesn't want us to ignore the painful parts of our histories. No, the Fourth Commandment isn't God's blinders-on idea that your parents were perfect. Recognize your hurtful story, but don't celebrate it. Instead, learn from it, and look toward the freedom that comes when you forgive your parents.

Forgiveness is God's difficult-lovely-necessary-holy gift. It's yours through Jesus' sacrifice on the cross.

And it's also yours to give your mom and dad.

THOUGHTS ABOUT THIS COMMANDMENT

1. The explanation of the Fourth Commandment says, "We should fear and love God so that we do not despise or anger our parents and other authorities, but honor them, serve and obey them, love and cherish them." Talk about the words *honor*, *serve*, *obey*, *love*, and *cherish*. These are action verbs. The stories on the following pages show how we can learn to do all these. Before the stories, let's talk about the slight differences between these words. How is honor different from serving and obeying? What about holding your parents in love and esteem? Is that easier than honoring, serving, or obeying? Tell the story of your family. Which of these is hardest for you?

2. In this commandment, God makes it clear that our relationship with our parents is very important. Luther's explanation shows this too. When you read the commandment and his explanation, how does obedience to this commandment feel? Challenging? Impossible? Or is it a joy to honor, obey, love, and serve your parents? Explain.

Family Honor & Family Armor

And Peter said to them, "Repent and be baptized every one of you in the name of Jesus Christ for the forgiveness of your sins, and you will receive the gift of the Holy Spirit. For the promise is for you and for your children and for all who are far off, everyone whom the Lord our God calls to Himself."

—the evangelist Luke in Acts 2:38–39

I'M WRITING THIS FROM MY MOM'S HOSPITAL ROOM. She's recovering from pneumonia and is expected to be released later today. My dad is at home, making sure her prescriptions are filled and the refrigerator is stocked with foods she can eat. This scene—my mom in the hospital right by my house in Katy, Texas, my parents *living* in Katy, and me helping care for them—is not at all where I imagined my family would be right now.

For the past twenty years, my parents lived eight hundred miles away in Leavenworth, Kansas. We shared the same kind of relationship as many adults who have never lived near one another. Love, sure. Honor, kind of. Like? Who knows? Our lives didn't intersect much.

The distance had served as armor, good for protecting us from a deeper relationship. We saw each other a few times a year for short visits. When we were done staying in each other's guest bedrooms, we went back to real life. If I worried my mom wasn't eating right or if my parents didn't agree with how many Christmas gifts our kids got, no one said anything. Why rock the boat?

This attitude toward extended family wasn't rare in either my mom's heritage or my dad's. Both of them had left home for college and never moved back. They tried to stay connected to their parents and siblings, but their hometowns were filled with raw memories. In the midst of infidelity and alcoholism, my mom's parents had separated. My dad had lost both his parents before he was thirty.

Today I can understand the pain these histories must have caused both of my parents. But when I was growing up in their home, I learned only this clear message: living close to family is complicated—and painful.

As I became a wife and a mother, I followed these rules of my family legacy. My kids saw their relationship with their grandparents very much the same way I had seen mine: a signature on birthday cards, a long-distance call, a strange bedroom to sleep in on Christmas Eve.

Not all our family armor came from distance, though. Some of it came from our learned fear to talk about our history. When I was a little girl, my mom could be emotionally distant. My dad and I had never discussed dark seasons in his life.

I had let them down too, certainly. For years, I had hid behind an urgent to-do list and an expensive life. I have not been a great daughter. I hoped that lots to accomplish and lots of success would be both the excuse and salve for them. But again, we didn't talk about it.

And then, my dad had bypass surgery, my mom's rheumatoid arthritis got worse, and my parents started talking about moving to Katy. This scared me a little because I didn't know what life with my parents would be like. (Actually, I didn't really know my parents very well at all.)

Then, suddenly, their Kansas house sold, and they were moving to our town in a month. The thought of my mom and dad as part of our daily lives set off my internal sirens: what in the world did a real relationship with family look like?

I emailed an older friend whom I trusted and asked her for wisdom. For several Fridays in a row, she and I met at Barnes & Noble. I told her the stories of my family: happy stories about how both my dad and I love theology and about how I truly enjoy chatting with my mom. But I also told her the sad stories about my childhood. These stories still stung.

She listened and sympathized. She told me I was totally justified in being hurt. Then, gently, she told me I needed to forgive my folks for whatever they did or did not do. Honor and life together, she said, both start with forgiveness.

So, after generations of concealing and not feeling, my parents and I are learning a little bit about God's forgiveness and life together. We are learning to be honest and to admit our own shortcomings. We are inviting each other over for dinner, but more important, we are learning to say so when we don't feel like coming.

Let me tell you, family honor is so much better than family armor. Six months later, I can tell you that my parents living near us is my very favorite thing ever. Who knew? I love hearing my mom's familiar voice as she sings in our church choir. My kids ask to do their homework with Papa. I'm learning what it means to spend the day at the hospital, and my parents are learning their grandkids' favorite dinner spots.

Every day, in every interaction, God gives us more grace, more love, more second chances. Through millions of different ways—lunch after church, bedside moments during hospital stays, and saying the words "I'm sorry" and "I'm here for you"—we are living together. We are learning that families are complicated and painful and so, so beautiful. And forgiveness is the necessary center of that knot.

Friends, I can tell you that God is right: a good relationship with our parents is so much more important than any of us want to believe.

Your parents weren't perfect; neither were mine. But they probably tried the best they could, and your new life together starts with forgiveness.

YOUR STORY/GOD'S STORY

1. Most of our family histories include disappointment. Name a couple of ways this has been true for your family. Where do you see sin's hold on generations in your own family? What generational "curses" has your family been susceptible to?

2. Read Isaiah 59:2; Matthew 6:12; and Ephesians 1:7. The chance to forgive your earthly parents is a blessing from your heavenly Father. He is clear that forgiveness is important to every part of our lives, especially for our most significant relationships. Have you forgiven your folks? What's your confession or testimony here?

3. The first three commandments define our relationship with God. The Fourth Commandment is the first with God's instructions about how we should treat others. Why do you think God begins this section with a commandment about the relationship with our parents?

4. Take a new look at yourself and your relationship with your parents by checking out Romans 7:4–5 and 2 Corinthians 5:16–21. We are alive in Christ, a new creation through Him. This is so hard for us to understand, but it is the very best news because it means we are no longer defined by sin. Our identity as sinners is forgiven because Jesus gives us a new identity through His death on our behalf. We bear the fruit of that. How does knowing you are forgiven affect the way you see the future of your family?

5. Luther tells us we should hold our parents in love and esteem. Talk about how forgiving our parents is an act of love toward them. Is it also an act of love toward God?

PRAY . . .

Dear Lord, You are my perfect, loving, and gracious Father. Help me to forgive my earthly father and mother. Help me to better honor and love my mom and dad. Thank You for sending Your Son, Jesus, to die in my place so I am forgiven and can forgive. In His redeeming name. Amen.

Knitting Lessons

Train up a child in the way he should go; even when he is old he will not depart from it.

—Solomon in Proverbs 22:6

My husband, Mike, comes from a close-knit extended family. His mom, Marcilee, and her sister, Judy, are best friends. Growing up, Mike's first and closest friends were his cousins. Their families gathered at Grandma's house for every holiday. Christmas and Easter, yes, but they also cooked pancakes together on Palm Sunday, cooked chili and cinnamon rolls on Halloween, and had a big picnic on Memorial Day. Every day, in a million different ways, Mike learned that God knits families together forever.

As the years wore on and Mike's generation married and had their own kids, he and his brothers got busy and missed lots of holidays at Grandma's house. But not his cousins—especially Chris, the middle son in Judy's family. Chris came to his nieces' and nephews' birthday parties. He didn't love boating or the lake, but he attended the family Fourth of July party every year anyway. If the family was together, Chris showed up.

In an age when families keep in touch through FaceTime and Facebook, Judy's family made it a priority to live face-to-face. For years, Chris worked as a legislative aide for a state senator, and he lived near his brother, sister, mom, and dad. Their family met for lunch after church on Sundays. They went on multigenerational family trips.

Watching them was watching a family live out the Fourth Commandment. This was what God meant about blessing generations through this commandment. They like being together. They are one another's best friends. Their family is close-knit—and knitting them together is love, forgiveness, memories, shared DNA, and deep respect for one another.

Knit deep into the fabric of their family is also honor. Over and over, Chris, his brother, Steve, and his sister, Anne, put aside their own schedules to spend time with their parents. Even as this family worked through difficult seasons—job changes, car accidents, and sickness—they remained close. As Mike and I began our own family, I realized how much each of them must sacrifice to keep these relationships intact. I was in awe.

On January 8, 2015, Marcilee called with the worst news of our lives. During a manic episode, Chris had jumped from his high-rise apartment balcony and died instantly.

For years, Chris had been fighting a private battle with bipolar syndrome. We hadn't realized that sweet, generous Chris had been struggling with mental illness.

As Mike and I flew to Nebraska for the funeral, we prayed and wondered what we would find in Lincoln. How could Chris's parents, his grandma, his brother and sister, and his nieces and nephew possibly make it through the next few days—the next several *years*—without Chris?

When Mike and I pulled up to the funeral home for the visitation, we were stony and silent. Each of us was just beginning the long grieving process for his cousin. And we were both scared, not knowing what would greet us or what to say to his family.

We shouldn't have worried. The knitting God had done in their lives was holding them together at their very hardest moment. As hundreds of mourners filed into the funeral home, Chris's family stood shoulder to shoulder to greet them.

The urn containing Chris's ashes rested near his family while a slide show of photographs flashed above their heads. In every picture—including the picture in front of us, of this strong family standing in the funeral home—their love and sacrifice were evident. Their family standing together by that urn was the picture of the Fourth Commandment.

The years of sacrifice, of honor, of love for one another had taught them exactly what to do in the face of tragedy: sacrifice your own agenda, show up, stand together, hold one another up, and trust and love God. Their strength and solidarity in the wake of Chris's death is the strongest testament to family honor I have ever seen.

This is also a strong testament to how much God loves families. When He designed the human race, He intentionally placed families at the center. We are not created through dust. God does not clone us. God involves our parents in the most nitty-gritty ways of birthing us and growing us as people.

Trust that the family you are a part of is our Creator's intentional design. He gave you the parents you have for a reason. He wants you to honor them because of the lessons you learn, but also because of the importance of that relationship.

April 10 was Chris's birthday, and it's also National Siblings Day. Chris's family arranged their schedules to go to a baseball game and honor Chris, who loved to watch sports. Even though the family probably had other things to do that night, they all showed up.

Chris's siblings and their spouses huddled together and basked in their love for one another. They celebrated God's gift of family and His grace that lets them keep loving one another, even when they missed Chris terribly. They hugged one another, took selfies together, and thanked God for their memories of Chris. They sat together in honor and lived out God's knitting lessons in the Fourth Commandment.

Just as Chris would have done.

YOUR STORY/GOD'S STORY

1. Our families are perhaps the very most important earthly gift God gives us. Talk about the knitting lessons you've learned in your family. How has your family supported one another in unique ways only they could?

2. Is it harder for us to honor our parents now than it was thousands of years ago, when God first gave this commandment? Or are the struggles the same? Look at these Bible verses to understand the ancient command God gives your family: Proverbs 23:22; Colossians 3:20; and Ephesians 6:1–4. How do we still struggle to follow this commandment?

3. In Galatians 6:7–10, Paul reminds us that we reap what we sow. We will reap the harvest "in due season" and "if we do not give up." What harvest are you waiting to reap in your parents, your siblings, your kids, or your extended family? How does God keep you strong when you want to give up?

4. Think of your favorite Bible story in Genesis. Talk about how God always preserves the family, even through hard times. Look at the details of this story. What lessons of love and sacrifice did these people learn through God keeping their families intact?

5. Part of the explanation of this commandment is that we should serve our parents. Talk about how you can serve yours by making time for them.

PRAY . . .

Heavenly Father, You love families and graciously protect and sustain them. So often, I devalue my parents and do a terrible job honoring them. Thank You for sending Your very own Son to die so I can understand what true love looks like. In His redeeming name. Amen.

You Will (Probably)
Turn into Your Mother

Do not be deceived: God is not mocked, for whatever one sows, that will he also reap. For the one who sows to his own flesh will from the flesh reap corruption, but the one who sows to the Spirit will from the Spirit reap eternal life.

—Paul in Galatians 6:7–8

IT SEEMS LIKE MOST OF MY FRIENDS are turning into their moms. (I am too.) Sometimes on Facebook, I confuse whole generations of women with each other. I do double takes when I'm scrolling through my feed. "Chelsea's mom looks so young. Oh, wait. That *is* Chelsea."

And no matter how hard we try *not* to, we seem to copy the exact parts of our moms we never liked in the first place. The equation is strangely inverse here. The more we dislike something about our own parents, the more likely we will grow up to be the same way. Also, the more likely our own kids will copy these same habits.

When I was a little girl, my best friend's mom was our Sunday School teacher. In the fifth grade, she sat us girls down and warned us that if we got pregnant before we were married, she would never forgive us.

Wait. What was she talking about? I had no idea *how* to get pregnant. I don't think anyone else did either. But we nodded because our teacher had tears in her eyes, and we understood that this was serious.

When her daughter, my best friend, started dating, her mother threatened her constantly, "If you get pregnant, you will be in trouble forever."

You probably know the rest of the story. On prom night, my best friend told me she was pregnant. We cried and hugged and talked about the wedding she had already begun planning. I wanted to ask, "How in the world did this happen? What about all your mom's warnings? You knew better."

Years later, I found out her mom had also gotten pregnant when she was eighteen.

Oh.

Another friend grew up hating his dad's anger. His dad had a stressful job, came home late, and then yelled at his kids. When they heard his car pull into the garage, they retreated to their rooms. As soon as his dad walked in the door, the mood of the whole house soured.

My friend vowed he would never be a dad like that. He turned down high-paying jobs and refused to follow the rat race to big paychecks. Instead, he was a teacher who left work at four o'clock to coach his kids' soccer practices. He tucked his kids in every night with bedtime stories he had written himself.

But then his wife got sick and needed several surgeries. My dear friend took a high-paying job to cover her medical expenses. He worked longer and longer hours and tried not to bring his stress home with him.

The last time we really talked, he told me how tired he was. He said he had been so short-tempered lately. He heard himself yelling at his kids for not picking up their clothes, for not coming for dinner, and for not finishing their homework—and he sounded just like his dad.

Somehow, by osmosis, kids pick up the worst habits of their parents. They imitate their parents' most dysfunctional relationships. Even if we don't understand how this happens, this truth remains: you will probably turn into your mother, and your kids will probably turn into you.

When it comes to growing family gardens, we often grow weeds. Or we overprune the healthy parts and overfertilize the weeds. Left to our own plans, we make a mess out of mothering.

But God tells us to entrust our children to Him. He tells you to root your family in the wisdom of His Word and faith from the Holy Spirit. This is how you grow the kind of family He intended.

Isn't this what we're all trying to do with our kids? Grow the kind of families that God tells us to? Yes, our best lessons about eating right and safe driving probably won't stick. Our kids will repel what we push them toward and what we force into their lives. They will pick up our most disgusting habits and have the same heartbreaks we do in such identical ways that it will feel eerie.

But here's what we can do: We can introduce them to their Savior. We can do our most honorable jobs as moms and show them how Jesus changes hearts. This is, really, the only honorable lesson that will make a difference.

Yes, I'm turning into my mother. Yes, my daughters will probably turn into me. Your kids are turning into you.

But that's okay because God is changing our hearts all the time. He is teaching the next generation important lessons of grace and how to love one another like He wants us to. Living as an honorable mom means living out those lessons as the Holy Spirit keeps turning our dying hearts into thriving ones.

YOUR STORY/GOD'S STORY

1. How do you see yourself turning into your mother and your kids turning into you? Where do you see God in this, and what's His command?

2. When we try to raise kids independent from God, we do not raise the families He intended. As a mom, where have you ignored God? What happened?

3. Knowing your kids are picking up so many of your habits, opinions, and mistakes can seem like an enormous amount of pressure and even guilt. How do you know God will give you strength for this? Read Isaiah 41:10; John 14:27; and Psalm 46:1–3.

4. Read 2 Timothy 1:5–7 about Eunice and Lois. Although Lois was a devout believer, her daughter, Eunice, didn't always honor her mother or God. Yet Paul tells us that it is through them that Timothy knew the Scriptures well. He went on to become one of the greatest pastors in the Early Christian Church. Talk about how this shows the importance of sharing God's truth with your kids and grandkids.

5. Think about yourself as a mother and Luther's words about this com-

mandment. Share some ideas about how you can live so your kids can honor and obey you.

PRAY . . .

Heavenly Father, You are my example of perfect love. As a mom, I fail to show true love to my kids. Forgive me for the ways I mess up, and help me to be an honorable mom by sharing Your love with the next generation. Help me to share Jesus and His love with my kids. In His redeeming name. Amen.

Salute the Uniform

*Let all bitterness and wrath and anger and clamor and slander be
put away from you, along with all malice. Be kind to one another,
tenderhearted, forgiving one another, as God in Christ forgave you.*

—Paul in Ephesians 4:31–32

PERHAPS THIS IS THE EXACT POINT, the precise intersection, where Christians who want to live the Ten Commandments stall: the cross section of abusive parents and the Fourth Commandment. Is God really asking us to honor the worst kind of parent, the cruel one? This command feels tone deaf and a little dangerous.

Let me tell you about my dear friend Ruthie. Over the years of watching her, I see how God can jump-start your life and help keep you from stalling at this painful intersection.

I met Ruthie at the school where I worked when I was a young teacher. She had just married her husband. She and her husband, Titus, were so in love, so hopeful, and so excited for their new life together.

During long talks over grilled cheese while monitoring lunch duty, Ruthie and I became friends and told our stories to each other. Her life hadn't been easy. She was from a remote Colorado farm town. Her mother was a pediatrician, and her dad homeschooled her. For several years, while Ruthie's mom was at work, her dad had molested her.

When Ruthie went to the University of Houston for college, her parents also moved there. She met Titus there, and as they fell in love, Ruthie told Titus what her dad had done. With his help, she eventually confronted her mom and dad. Right around the time Ruthie and Titus were getting married, they were also doing some deep, difficult work with her parents and her past.

Even though Ruthie's dad admitted to what he had done, he didn't accept her anger or agree to see a Christian counselor with her. Ruthie's mom became stoic and refused to talk about it. On her wedding day, Ruthie began her life with her husband and ended her life with her parents. She left for her honeymoon and decided she could never see them again.

For the next year, Ruthie tried both to nurture her young marriage and heal from her childhood. Throughout the school year, she would show up for faculty devotions with her blue eyes bloodshot from crying and lack of sleep. She emailed me long, angry messages about what God had let happen—but when I emailed her back, Titus called and said she didn't want to talk about this.

Eventually, Ruthie left the job and we lost contact. I heard she had a daughter. I missed Ruthie and thought about her often, hoping she had found some relief from her past.

Then one day, Ruthie called with happy news. Her mom had contacted her and apologized for how she had reacted. She wanted to know her granddaughter. When she told Ruthie's dad she wanted a relationship with her daughter and granddaughter, he told her to leave. Ruthie's mom asked her if she could live with them. She would take care of her granddaughter, and Ruthie could go back to teaching.

Ruthie was so excited about this. She had her mom back, and she could share her daughter with her. Little by little, Ruthie and her mom talked about what had happened. Her mom apologized for shutting her out, and Ruthie forgave her. She emailed me about the new teaching job she had, and she sounded so happy. I was so happy for her too.

Ruthie's dad was not happy. He called her mom constantly and told her he loved her. He said he would do anything: the counseling, make a relationship with Ruthie, whatever it took to have his wife back.

Eventually, Ruthie's mom went back to him. She said she still loved him and didn't believe in divorce. When Ruthie tried to talk to her, she became stony again.

Ruthie started emailing me and asking me hard questions about what to do next. How could she honor a father who had abused her or a mother who had abandoned her when she needed her—twice? Did God really want her to honor such toxic parents?

I didn't know what to tell her. I had started a moms Bible study at our church, and I asked Ruthie to come. She did come, and through the study, we started learning so much about what God intended for parenthood. We learned that parenthood is not a consumer relationship; it's a covenant one. In other words, we don't choose our parents, and we can't trade them or end our relationship with them.

Through long meetings over fajitas and frozen yogurt, Ruthie and I talked about this. Yes, her parents had messed up on more levels and in more ways than she could understand. Yes, she disliked them and the way they treated her. Yes, she wanted to punish them.

It was natural for Ruthie to hate her parents. But God was calling her to the supernatural, to forgiveness and honor.

As she was starting to see, she couldn't take these steps on her own. Only through the power of the Holy Spirit could she forgive them. Only the Holy Spirit could soften her heart. Only the Holy Spirit could heal what had happened in her childhood.

Ruthie prayed to forgive her parents, and God transformed their relationship. She calls honoring her parents "saluting the uniform." Although they had damaged her in the deepest ways, they were still the mom and dad God had given her. The best news Ruthie learned was that she was not responsible for changing her parents.

And neither are you. If your mom and dad were abusive, neglectful, hateful, angry, or played favorites, this is not how God wanted them to parent you. But you are off the hook for transforming their hearts. That is God's job.

As God works in their hearts and yours, salute the uniform. Understand that figuring out how to honor disappointing parents is a lifelong process, but God will give you the patience, forgiveness, and gentleness to salute their honorable place in your life.

YOUR STORY/GOD'S STORY

1. What less-than-honorable habits did your parents have? How can you show respect for their vocations rather than for their actions?

See Ephesians 4:14–15; Romans 13:1–2; and Titus 3:1.

2. Honor is different from liking. Liking is based on emotion, and emotion changes all the time. Honoring is based on something deeper. Honoring is a promise to not give up on your parents. In what ways are you trying to honor your parents right now? How is this going?

3. Read Romans 8:12–17. Honoring your parents is often a dance between dark moments and light moments. During the dark moments, it feels like it will be dark forever. We forget that the Lord is in the miracle business and we are no longer slaves to sin. What's the good news here about our relationships now that we're God's adopted children?

4. Read Galatians 5:22–23. God gives you so many second (third, fourth, fifth, zillion) chances with your parents. What's your prayer for your relationship with them? What do you have faith God will do?

5. Luther says we should not despise our parents. If there is something they've done that you despise, how can you move forward to forgive them, give them honor, and hold them in love and esteem?

PRAY . . .

Father, when I look at You, I can see how perfect Your love is. Help me forgive my parents for the ways they've hurt me. Change my heart from bitterness to graciousness. Help me to see that through Jesus, total forgiveness is possible. In His redeeming name. Amen.

Do Not Kill

"You shall not murder."

—God's command to His people in Exodus 20:13

"You have heard that it was said to those of old, 'You shall not murder; and whoever murders will be liable to judgment.' But I say to you that everyone who is angry with his brother will be liable to judgment; whoever insults his brother will be liable to the council; and whoever says, 'You fool!' will be liable to the hell of fire."

—Jesus in Matthew 5:21–22

THE FIFTH COMMANDMENT IS LIKE AN ICEBERG. Most of the time, we see only the tiny, sharp point poking above the calm surface of polite society. We believe this commandment is for only a small group of people, an instruction God gives to the worst of the worst—serial killers, mass shooters, and terrorists who are living in pitch-black darkness.

But then Jesus shows the deeper part of this commandment, and we see the huge, ugly mountain of hate that's hidden in all of us. It goes on and on, a Mount Everest of our anger, complacency, and revenge.

Jesus says we're all guilty of the sins that keep us from getting along with one another. Selfishness and hate are as much a part of our human hearts as the four chambers are.

The Fifth Commandment doesn't stop even there. It keeps revealing more and more of our sin. Jesus also tells us that we can't be nonchalant about those who are dying. Every single human is made in His image, and it's a big deal when even one life is lost. Jesus tells us that if people are dying when we could help them, we're also guilty of murder.

Before you give up on the Fifth Commandment, shut this book, and leave to play Candy Crush, hold on. This commandment is also full of good news and God's love. You don't have to keep that boulder of anger in your soul, and you'll feel a lot better when it's gone. Just as God forgives us, He also tells us to forgive. His love and grace can clean that sick sludge out of your soul like one of those magic bleach tricks.

God knows this is what we all need, and in this commandment, He tells us to stop choosing hate and let His seeds of bleach-white grace grow in our hearts. His grace and forgiveness melt our mountain of hate like hot chocolate syrup melts a mound of ice cream.

Forgiveness is God's miracle gift for us. This was the gift He gave us when He sent His Son to die for us. Jesus lived a perfect life—He never let this iceberg of hate take root in His soul—and then He died on the cross to save us from our own sick selves.

The best news? His death and resurrection turn our mountains of hate into mountains of His perfect love. His sacrifice on the cross gives us perfect hope.

THOUGHTS ABOUT THIS COMMANDMENT

1. The Fifth Commandment is a huge, encompassing commandment, and Luther's explanation shows this. He says, "We should fear and love God so that we do not hurt or harm our neighbor in his body, but help and support him in every physical need." In our discussion, we'll look at all the ways we hurt others (physically, emotionally, and spiritually). Think about your relationships right now. Which ones are hardest for you? What weapons have you used to hurt these people?

2. Really? Befriend the people we don't like? Help them with every one of their needs? Are there certain, difficult relationships where these seem impossible? Tell your worst stories of cruelty and grudges.

Sick Revenge

Beloved, never avenge yourselves, but leave it to the wrath of God, for it is written, "Vengeance is Mine, I will repay, says the Lord."

—Paul in Romans 12:19

LINDY IS ONE OF MY LIFELONG BEST FRIENDS, and Finley is her daughter. Finley is a gorgeous, funny, curious, loving six-year-old who happens to have an extra chromosome.

Lindy didn't know about Finley's extra chromosome until the day after she was born. The prenatal screenings hadn't detected it, and even at birth, the doctors didn't realize Finley was special. Twenty-four hours after Lindy gave birth to her long-awaited first child, a pediatrician gently announced that Finley had Down syndrome.

Lindy felt like she had been punched in the gut. Special-needs diagnoses are always life changing. A birth diagnosis is really, really hard.

Lindy and her husband, Kevin, had to process all their emotions in fast-forward. They had to quickly grieve the typical child they had planned. They needed to embrace Finley, the helpless newborn who waited for their full love, dedication, and attention.

The hours that followed Finley's diagnosis were the most vulnerable of Lindy's life. What did Down syndrome mean, exactly? Did she have the patience and tenderness to mother a special-needs child? Could she love a child so radically different from what she had expected? How could she possibly provide everything Finley needed?

In these fragile, horrible hours of doubt, Kevin stepped up. He promised Lindy everything would be okay. He would make it okay. He would provide exactly what they needed to make sure this was the best family ever.

Lindy held on to Kevin's promises. They got her through the next terrible few days, when she would hold Finley and cry at what this diagnosis meant. And during the first few months, Lindy felt like all this would be okay. She had Kevin, a supportive sister and parents, and God. Maybe this would be easy.

It was not easy. Less than a year later, Lindy discovered text messages on Kevin's phone from a woman he was sleeping with. Kevin admitted that, yes, he was having an affair with one of his bosses at work. He didn't want to be a family anymore. He was moving out.

Lindy's life was falling apart again. Kevin had lied. He couldn't handle the pressure of this special family. To say Lindy had no respect for him would be an understatement. She hated him. She hated how he had made promises he couldn't keep. She hated how he lied to make everyone like him. She hated how sarcastic and mean he could get. And she still had to co-parent with him.

If anyone had a reason to make another person's life miserable, it was Lindy. She deserved revenge. Kevin had walked out for an easier life. He had left her holding his empty promises and Finley.

As Lindy's friends, we hated Kevin too—and we felt helpless. We wanted to fix this for her. We told her she could make Kevin pay. She could work it so Kevin never saw his daughter again. She had our permission to make his life very painful.

And, for a while, she did a little of that. During that first year after their divorce, Lindy yelled at Kevin, called him a failure, and told anyone who would listen what a disappointment he was.

No one blamed her for this. No one would have blamed Lindy if this ugly divorce had turned her into a victim. Who more than Lindy had a license for revenge? Life with Finley was exhausting, and Kevin was shacking up with the woman he had chosen over her. Kevin was a jerk, so she got to be the bitter ex-wife.

Maybe their divorce started out with those first seeds of hate, but God didn't leave her with those in her heart. He had a bigger story to tell her. Slowly, over several months, God gave Lindy hope. He gave her a group of mom friends who helped her navigate Finley's unique needs. She found a church with a program for special-needs kids. God gave her millions of little opportunities to see He was taking care of her, that He had promised her these good things.

Slowly, Lindy realized this truth: hating Kevin might feel good, but it fueled the worst part of her soul, the part she didn't want to be. Making his life miserable didn't change anything. More and more, she recognized that the Holy Spirit was the only one who really could change the parts of her life she really needed to have changed.

This is what Lindy has learned: God doesn't tell us to forgive because it's best for the other person, or even for Him. Forgiveness is best for us. It's best for us spiritually, but it's also best for us emotionally and physically.

Want proof? Mayo Clinic's website has a page about the physical symptoms of withholding forgiveness. The medical facts are that holding on to bitterness causes irritability, increases anxiety, depresses the immune system, and inflames the joints. These are medical facts.

God created our bodies, and He knows what damages us, what pricks our souls, what kills His seeds of love. Choosing hate over forgiveness hurts us on every level.

For Lindy, forgiveness was the difference between believing that God makes everything new and living in the murky, ugly, dirty place. Forgiveness, quite literally, changed Lindy's life. Now her story isn't one about villains, hurts, and revenge, but one about how God can help us forgive even the least-deserving people.

Lindy's story is a dramatic one of Jesus' victory over sin. It's the story of a little girl with Down syndrome who will grow up in a house full of love instead of hate. It's the story of everything Jesus did on the cross. It's the story of His all-consuming love for us.

And it is a very special story.

YOUR STORY/GOD'S STORY

1. Talk about someone you are totally justified in hating, a person who hurt you in a way that makes revenge seem like a really good idea. What's the rest of the story? Are you stuck in the hate? How is God working in your heart?

2. Think about the evil people in our world. How does God "take care" of them with revenge? Read John 15:7–14. Discuss the idea that the sin itself is the punishment. What did Kevin miss because of his bad decisions? What about Lindy's hate? How did this hurt her?

3. The hate in our hearts is the cancer, the black plague, the thick tar that seeps in and around our thoughts. When you hold grudges, lash out, live with bitterness, and refuse to forgive, you feed that toxic part of yourself. Talk about the physical symptoms of living with anger that you have noticed. Read Ephesians 4:25–32. How does Paul tell us to live?

4. Could you call forgiveness a miracle (something God does that we can't do on our own)? Why or why not? Read Ephesians 4:31–32. Where do we learn forgiveness?

5. Talk about ways withholding forgiveness causes bodily harm. What other kind of harm does it cause? What about spiritual damage? Considering this, what solution does God give us?

PRAY . . .

Dear Lord, I can look to You to see what real love looks like. Forgive me when I indulge my dirty heart and want to hurt others. Help me to focus my eyes on Jesus and His example of humble kindness and sacrificing love. In His redeeming name. Amen.

Everyone Has
a Mother-in-Law Story

Therefore, if anyone is in Christ, he is a new creation. The old has passed away; behold, the new has come.

—Paul in 2 Corinthians 5:17

YOUR MOTHER-IN-LAW IS a strange combination of both family (your most important, intimate clan) and foreigner (not someone you chose to be in that clan). In other words, your mother-in-law might be your trickiest relationship.

My friends joke about the Mother-in-Law Lottery. Perhaps you got a good one, who will respect your decisions, treat your husband like an adult, and help out with your kids. But maybe you got the other kind—one who has terrible boundaries, has no respect, and depends on your family to fill up her neediness.

My dear friend Amanda got the second type. When Amanda met her husband, David, she fell in love with his protective, nurturing, I'll-take-care-of-you personality. Caring for other people was his *thing*. Mostly, as she would come to learn, David took care of his mom, who was depressed, overweight, a chronic smoker, and needy.

David was born when she was sixteen. During his childhood, she married twice. When those men left, she clung to David. He was often caught in the middle of her bad boundaries. At an early age, he learned his most valuable role was to be his mom's caretaker.

Even after David married Amanda, he took care of his mom. She called their house at all hours, needing money, someone to listen to her, and cigarettes.

Amanda dreaded those calls. She tried to be sympathetic to the hard life David's mom had had, but she also needed space from her neediness. Amanda and David fought bitterly about his mom. Amanda felt like he was as addicted to helping his mom as she was to Coca-Cola and Camels. So when Amanda found out she was pregnant, she told David it was time to see that his most important roles were as father and husband and no longer as son.

One day while Amanda and David were looking at a townhouse for their new little family, David's mom started calling. David didn't answer the calls, even as his mom called again and again. He was trying to learn how to take care of his new family and also show his mom healthy boundaries.

His mom had been calling because she didn't feel well, and she died in her bedroom the next morning from congestive heart failure.

Obviously, this was not a great start to David and Amanda's marriage. David had failed at his first job, being his mom's savior. He felt like a disappointment, and he numbed that pain by getting high.

Amanda also struggled. She was ashamed that she hadn't liked his mom. She felt guilty that she had told David to choose his new family over his mother. And she was angry about the hold David's mom still had on him. David's demons with drugs came from that relationship, and now those demons were haunting their new family.

If God had left David and Amanda right there, their story would've ended in disaster and divorce. But the Holy Spirit was working in both of their hearts. They didn't realize it, but He had big plans for this dysfunctional family.

Amanda's parents showed up and did the hardest work imaginable. They shared the Gospel with Amanda and with David. They loved their son-in-law, even when he was completely unlovable. Amanda's mom spent most of that season on her knees, asking God to intervene and give a fresh start to her daughter's family.

David moved into a Christian rehab facility, and Amanda prayed at home for their marriage. During that year, their pastor met with both of them. He talked to Amanda about letting God heal her from her guilt and anger about her mother-in-law as much as he talked to David about living clean and sober.

During this crazy, hard year, God softened their hearts. God transformed their relationship and laid down a new structure. From the ashes of their brokenness, David and Amanda built a family on His Word. Amanda now saw her mother-in-law differently. This woman had had her own demons, but she had raised one of the kindest, most nurturing, and honest men in the world. Months later, Amanda gave David a gift. A key to their house. He was coming home.

That was twelve years ago, and Amanda still tells this story as a testimony of how God changes lives. God gave them second, fourth, six-hundredth chances. In turn, David and Amanda gave each other second, fourth, and six-hundredth chances.

In Amanda's living room is a large picture of her mother-in-law. Amanda is the first one to tell visitors what her mother-in-law did right. Even though she wasn't perfect, she was David's mom. And she did the very best she could.

Maybe you're also inside the drama of a bad relationship with your mother-in-law. Maybe she's cruel or has terrible boundaries or buys your kids too much stuff. Maybe you wish you could change her to be someone who fits into your ideal family. Maybe you dislike the ways she's not like your mom, the ways she treats your husband, or how she acted at your wedding twenty years ago.

I don't have daughters-in-law yet, but I'm guessing those relationships are pretty hard for mothers-in-law too. In-laws demand forgiveness for "unforgivable" sins—intentional or otherwise—against our families.

Jesus tells us that holding a grudge against your mother-in-law is the same as stabbing her. Harboring resentment for her bad behavior a decade ago is just as bad as adding cyanide to her morning coffee. This is God's way: Forgive her for every one of her crimes against you and against your family. And then feel the relief in your soul.

God can, and will, change our difficult families. Maybe He'll work through a year of rehab and Bible study. Or maybe it will happen faster than that, as soon as you finish reading this and call your mother-in-law to ask for her forgiveness.

After God's heart-softening and forgiving, you will also have a testimony of how He worked a miracle right in the ugliest, hardest part of your messy family life.

That testimony will be a story about the grace that's ours to share, thanks to Jesus' love and sacrifice on the cross.

YOUR STORY/GOD'S STORY

1. Tell your mother-in-law/daughter-in-law story. Has this been a difficult relationship for you? How has God redeemed your anger for His good? Where do you still need His love?

2. Read Ephesians 4:26–27. Paul tells us to not let the sun go down on our anger because it gives the devil a foothold. Where is this happening in your life right now? What anger is opening a door in your soul for the devil to come in and whisper lies to you?

3. Read the story of Ruth and Naomi in Ruth 1. How did God work through Ruth's relationship with her mother-in-law to change her heart? How was Ruth flexible to His work? What different decision could Ruth have made?

4. Read Galatians 5:22–23. How is the fruit of the Spirit different from the fruits of Satan? Where do you see both in your toughest relationships, with difficult in-laws, rebellious children, or a co-worker you don't like?

5. In our relationships with our in-laws, we have a unique opportunity to help and befriend those whom God has placed in our lives. How can you do this with your in-laws?

PRAY . . .

Heavenly Father, You love equally and completely. Help me to follow Your command to love and forgive, even in my hardest relationships. Help me to show the grace Jesus showed to every single person when He died for our sins. In His redeeming name. Amen.

Spiritual Antibiotics

Refrain from anger, and forsake wrath! Fret not yourself; it tends only to evil. For the evildoers shall be cut off, but those who wait for the LORD shall inherit the land.

—David in Psalm 37:8–9

I'LL CALL THESE PAST FEW MONTHS the Summer of Anger because there's no other way to name whatever has been going on with our two boys. All of a sudden, both of my young sons are mad at the world. My oldest is eight years old, and my youngest is five years old, and living with them is like living with miniature Andy Roddicks.

Case in point: Nate, our five-year-old, started biting himself because he was "so mad." Throughout this summer, he walked around with half-moon teeth circles on his knees and arms. We told him he couldn't do this, but he explained that when he got angry, he *had* to hurt something.

Sam, our eight-year-old, suddenly felt rage whenever he couldn't get others to cooperate or listen to him. We could see (and hear) his desperation because he broke down in feral cries every time his sisters blocked his way or took the last pencil. We never knew when his temper tantrums were coming, but let me tell you, our neighbors two houses down could hear them.

Where had our mild-mannered boys gone? I didn't know how to handle these tantrums. Should I hug them or punish them?

Mike and I talked to our friends about what "normal" anger for a kid looked like. The reports from the trenches were not good. Other parents told horror stories of their own kids throwing hour-long temper tantrums about having to wear socks or turn off the TV.

I heaped punishments on the boys, but that didn't help. By the time the Summer of Anger drew to a close and we were shopping for school supplies, I had had enough. We had to fix this before school started. Angry kids are the ones who punch girls at recess and tell the teacher she's stupid.

One afternoon, Sam and I were part of a particularly harrowing scene in the school supply aisle at Target. Sam wanted to pick out his school supplies in peace, but Nate wanted his attention and wouldn't stop kicking him.

"STOP!" Sam screamed over and over.

"Stop screaming!" I said to Sam over and over. "Stop kicking," I told Nate, doling out punishments every time he kicked. No desserts. No swimming this afternoon. Earlier bedtime for both of them.

Then Sam just lost it. He started the feral screams. "I am so tired of my brother! I can't do this anymore! No one loves me!" He collapsed beside the cart and started crying.

I felt just as desperate as Sam looked. Why so much anger? What in the world had we done wrong to get to this?

Tears were in my eyes too. I knelt next to Sam. Other shoppers avoided our aisle. I'm sure someone was about to go for the security guard. I didn't care.

"You feel like you're not loved? Why not?" I asked. "I love you so much. Don't you know that?"

"NO!" Sam answered. "When no one listens to me, no one loves me. When things don't happen like I want, no one loves me. I know your secret. You really don't want to take care of me."

"What are you talking about?" I asked. "This is how you feel?"

He nodded. "That's why I am so mad!"

"Sam, what does God want you to know about this—right now?"

He thought for a long time. The other kids were getting tired of looking at spirals and were dancing around the cart. "He wants me to know that He loves me."

"YES!" I said. "He does! What else?"

"That He will take care of me?"

"He will!"

Right here. These were the two lessons the Summer of Anger taught me.

What Sam said on the floor that day made so much sense: these were the two reasons the boys had been getting mad all summer.

The first lesson was that every single person gets angry every day. You and I might not become screaming feral cats when we get cut off in traffic, but the same emotion is there. We are prideful people and hate it when life suddenly conflicts with our agenda.

The second lesson was exactly what Sam said as he sat next to our cart at Target. We all get angry because we're basically very afraid. We're afraid we won't have enough of what we need. Even when we tell the world we're fine, we're stuffing our mouths with food or wine or stuffing our closet with clothes or stuffing our minds with lies. We are all trying to fill up the holes we feel inside.

Deep, deep down we all need more security, something to make us feel tethered to care and love. Most of us are missing a very important balm, and we are desperate to get it back. Maybe we're not biting ourselves, but we have a low-grade restlessness—an anger—in our souls.

None of us wants to live like this. Anger feels uncomfortable, like wearing an atomic heat suit. No one ever gives TED talks about what a great idea it is to live with rage brewing inside yourself.

So, the next few times I got really angry, I didn't react. Instead, I asked myself why I was angry. Sam was right. At the moment I'm angry, I believe I am not loved enough. What a crazy, horrible lie to believe.

Now my anger—and my sons' anger—makes more sense. None of us are budding psychopaths; we are all just human. The solution was not to confine the boys so they could totally avoid frustrating situations; the solution was to teach them they are loved, that they don't have to get angry. The solution was to keep reminding them of their Savior. This was the spiritual antibiotic our boys needed to kill their rage infection.

Through Jesus, God is always offering us the spiritual antibiotics we need for our anger. He is always telling me He loves me and that I'm made holy through the sacrifice of my Savior, that Son He gave up to suffering and death and hell because He loves me so much.

Every single second of every single day, God shows me He is taking care of me. His love is my message—my spiritual antibiotics—to share with the world.

YOUR STORY/GOD'S STORY

1. In the next hour or day, you will feel angry. What will cause this? What are your hot buttons? What does Jesus want you to know about this?

2. Our solution to the low-grade anger problem is to live in seclusion. Martin Luther pointed out that while this might keep us comfortable, we're really just avoiding the problem of our hateful hearts. Talk about how you're tempted to build a monastery to keep yourself away from people who make you angry. Read James 4:1–2. What deep spiritual balm do you need from God right now? Why are you not asking Him for this?

3. Every person you meet is fighting a hard battle. They are doing the best they can to be brave. The people you see are trying to be stoic, but they have gaping soul wounds and are really lost. How can you share God's love? Read Romans 12:14–18.

4. Read Matthew 5:23–24. Jesus teaches hard lessons about what forgiveness really looks like. How does your relationship with others also affect your relationship with God?

5. As Luther said in his explanation of this commandment, our neighbors (the barista who makes your espresso, the guy who shot you the finger when you cut him off in traffic, and your actual neighbors) need us to help and befriend them. Are there some small and big ways you can incorporate this into your day?

PRAY . . .

Gracious Lord, Your patience never runs out. Forgive my anger when I lash out at others. Help me share Your medicinal love and healing grace with the world that needs it. Thank You for the example of Jesus, who perfectly modeled righteous anger and righteous love. In His redeeming name. Amen.

The African
Children's Choir

"Then the righteous will answer Him, saying, 'Lord, when did we see You hungry and feed You, or thirsty and give You drink? And when did we see You a stranger and welcome You, or naked and clothe You? And when did we see You sick or in prison and visit You?'
"And the King will answer them, 'Truly, I say to you, as you did it to one of the least of these My brothers, you did it to Me.'"

—Jesus in Matthew 25:37–40

A COUPLE OF YEARS AGO, our church tried a radically different kind of VBS. Instead of the usual crafts and games, the African Children's Choir came to our church to teach our kids Bible stories, praise songs, and about life in Uganda. Two of the girls, Nina and Patience, were staying at our house. Our family couldn't wait.

If you've heard the African Children's Choir, you know what a treat this was for our family. These boys and girls travel from African countries to hundreds of churches all over the world to give concerts and meet families. On the last night of our VBS, the kids from Memorial Lutheran would get to perform a huge concert with the African Children's Choir. We invited all of Houston.

After the choir tours the world, the kids go back to their home country to attend school. Through donations, each child now has a lifelong scholarship for an outstanding education. These children become doctors, teachers, engineers, and lawyers. They stay in Africa to make changes to help its poorest citizens.

The program is remarkable because of who these children are. The African Children's Choir chooses the choir based on need. These are the children who have the most dismal futures of literally anyone in the world. Most have lost parents to AIDS. Many have been abused and have no access to proper nutrition or safe water. Without the African Children's Choir, their lives would be miserable if not impossible.

We prepared our kids for the visitors coming to stay at our house. We warned them not to ask about the kids' families so they wouldn't have to tell their painful stories. We didn't want the choir kids to feel awkward.

We shouldn't have worried. Nina and Patience and our kids all spoke the universal language of Kid. Giggling happens in every language, and that's what they all did over silly songs, playing keep-away in the pool, and spending hours at the park. The kids fell in love with one another.

When Nina and Patience boarded their bus to travel to the next church, we all cried. We would miss them so much, and it was hard to let them go. I felt like the week had been a tremendous success. Our kids had learned the important lesson that people are the same across the world.

Naively, I believed this was the only lesson our kids had learned.

But the week with the African Children's Choir had changed them in ways I didn't see at first. Our kids had attended the concerts and heard the heartbreaking stories. They were old enough to understand that Nina and Patience came from terrible poverty. Our children were not only sympathetic, but they were also angry about this.

Why did Nina and Patience have to walk so far to get water? Why didn't everyone in Uganda get to go to school? What is AIDS? Why did Nina and Patience have to go back to a country where they weren't safe?

We tried to explain how complicated international poverty is and the challenges of getting money to the people who need it most. We talked about how we had already donated to the African Children's Choir, and that our money would help give kids clean water, food, and an education.

But our kids wanted to give *all* our money to Uganda. More than that, they wanted to know why our family needed such a big house when Nina and Patience lived on dirt floors. They wanted to know why we needed new clothes when so many kids had none.

I dreaded these conversations because I had no good answers. At the same time, I was also reading more about international poverty. I learned that 780 million people do not have access to clean water. Malnutrition is the underlying cause of death for at least 3.1 million children every year.

Unbelievable.

I could not picture the enormity of what these numbers meant. I knew about the struggles in Africa in a theoretical way, but this hit me as a mother. Millions of mothers sent their kids to bed every night without enough to eat.

On an even deeper level, our kids were upset about the humanness of these numbers. They had fallen in love with Nina and Patience, and they realized each one of those millions of people had a story, had likes and dislikes, feelings, and emotions. These were not faceless multitudes. These were people who could be their friends—and they were dying because they didn't have the resources we took for granted.

During this time, I was also reading about the Fifth Commandment, and I understood a truth that made me even more uncomfortable. These people who were dying in Africa and India and Mexico were my responsibility. My children were right. People were dying because they lacked basic resources. And I was not doing enough to help them.

Here's what I was starting to understand: Every single human—the unborn, the old and disabled, the marginalized in other countries, the terrorists, and the thugs—is made in God's image. Every human life is God's best creation. Every single life is precious to Him. Every person's breath, soul, brain cycles, eyes, heart, and spirit are irreplaceable.

Human bodies are uniquely temples of the Holy Spirit. We are not smart animals, as evolutionists claim. Humans are different from squirrels or cats or pigs because God chose *us* to bear His image. We must do what we can to sustain every human life.

I didn't have to explain this to my kids because they already understood it. When they looked into Nina's and Patience's eyes, they saw souls just like theirs. They instantly understood the truth that God loves humans so much that He made us in His image.

It's been more than two years since the African Children's Choir stayed with us, but the tension of their visit is still part of our daily lives. I wish I could report we gave all our money to families who didn't have food for dinner. But we have not. I'm embarrassed at how little we have still done to help.

But we do have a new awareness now. Our children have a deep understanding of an idea that some adults never grasp: human life is sacred. God loves, treasures, and celebrates every single one.

The good news is that God loves and cares for each of these people individually. So even though the numbers can seem faceless to us, they are not to Him. He is intervening, caring, sustaining, saving, and showing His grace to every person constantly. Just like He does with me and you.

This good news doesn't let us off the hook, though. Not one bit. God is clear: We should care for those who have the least. We should share our clothes, our hospitality, our food, our water, and our money.

Most of all, we should share the Gospel with the world, with these billions of individual souls who need to know that "God shows His love for us in that while we were still sinners, Christ died for us" (Romans 5:8).

YOUR STORY/GOD'S STORY

1. Read 1 John 3:16–18; Matthew 5:16; and Luke 12:48. Share your favorite story of how God blessed you with the opportunity to bless someone else. How did you love in deed and not only in word?

2. Read Deuteronomy 15:10–11. Where do you struggle to help those who need it? Think about those dying in poverty, in abortion, in suicide, and in drug abuse. How could you help?

3. Read Matthew 25:35–40 and talk about the problem of poverty in our world. Why do you think God allows for some people to suffer while He gives so much to others? What should our reaction be?

4. Read Matthew 14:13–21 and Matthew 15:29–39. Why does Jesus feed the hungry people? What does Jesus teach us through this story about food and relationships? How did the multitudes experience love that day?

5. In Luther's explanation, he tells how we should help every person in their bodily needs. What physical needs do you see around you right now?

Is there something you could provide to help those who are hurting or dying?

PRAY . . .

Heavenly Father, You created everything in the universe, and You sustain every breathing creature. Forgive me when I don't help the dying or suffering. Open my heart to more compassion and more generosity. Help me to follow the example of Your perfect Son, Jesus, and His love. In His redeeming name. Amen.

Don't Commit Adultery

"You shall not commit adultery."

—God in Exodus 20:14

"You have heard that it was said, 'You shall not commit adultery.' But I say to you that everyone who looks at a woman with lustful intent has already committed adultery with her in his heart."

—Jesus in Matthew 5:27–30

THINK BACK TO YOUR LAST TRIP to the grocery store and choosing the best milk for your family. Maybe you stared at the dairy case, wondering if your family would drink milk from coconuts and if it was better than the stuff from cows. Maybe you should buy lactose-free. Chocolate? Cashew? Nonfat?

If it seems like all these choices are overwhelming, sociologists agree. We have more consumer choices than at any other time or any other people in history. Researchers say the power to choose changes what we believe about the choices we make and even about ourselves.

According to studies, people who are given dozens of options believe they're pickier than they actually are. We start seeing ourselves as extremely sensitive consumers who need lots of choices to meet our highly nuanced tastes. Offer us only one choice, and we feel restless, like we've been unjustly asked to settle.

Has living in the Land of Choices changed the way we see relationships too? Do we love our role as consumers so much that we've forgotten how to commit? And what about this: Does marriage to the same person every day for the rest of your life feel like settling? Does it make you restless?

Some days you might wish for an aisle full of husband options. If only he were a little better at listening, at tackling home-improvement projects, at taking you out on fun dates, at passion.

The world will tell you this kind of choosiness is wise and that you deserve a husband like this. You can be a consumer here too. Choose someone else, someone who caters to your highly sensitive needs. Don't settle for forever.

But God says committing is better than consuming. In the Sixth Commandment, He tells us that marriage matters. It's through this commandment that He gives us unique blessings—sex, children, complete oneness, and the lesson of how to forgive like Jesus did.

Through the commitment of marriage, God gives you more love, more strength, and more compassion than you ever thought possible. You learn that a good marriage is never about choosing the perfect person, but about becoming a more perfect person yourself. This is what makes a lifelong commitment work.

This is the commitment you'll celebrate when your grandkids dance around you at your fiftieth wedding anniversary. When you look in your husband's face, you will see the decades of this love, growth, sacrifice, strength, and for-giveness.

Most important, you will know that the love you're actually celebrating is the love of Christ. It's what carried you and taught you and surrounded you—and it's at the very heart of the Sixth Commandment.

THOUGHTS ABOUT THIS COMMANDMENT

1. The explanation for the Sixth Commandment makes it clear that the commandment includes every person—both single and married. Luther explains, "We should fear and love God so that we lead a sexually pure and decent life in what we say and do, and husband and wife love and honor each other." If you're not married, what does a pure life look like?

2. What does it look like to "love and honor" your husband? Talk about what sins can plant the seeds of adultery long before an actual, physical affair.

Pride Cometh
before the Affair

"Blessed are the poor in spirit, for theirs is the kingdom of
heaven. Blessed are those who mourn, for they shall be comforted.
Blessed are the meek, for they shall inherit the earth. Blessed are those
who hunger and thirst for righteousness, for they shall be satisfied.
Blessed are the merciful, for they shall receive mercy. Blessed are the pure
in heart, for they shall see God. Blessed are the peacemakers, for they
shall be called sons of God."

—Jesus in Matthew 5:3–9

GRACIE AND I HAD GONE TO CHURCH TOGETHER FOR YEARS, but we didn't
know each other well until we both started volunteering to clean the fellowship hall after Wednesday-night dinners. As we scrubbed tables and wrapped
up leftovers, we became friends. When I told her about this book and how I
didn't know what story I would use for the Sixth Commandment, she said she
knew what story I needed—hers. The next week we met for lunch, and she
told me her story.

Gracie and her husband, Lee, had always seemed like an exceptionally sweet
couple. That day at lunch, over shrimp quesadillas with mango salsa and tangy
Key lime pie, Gracie told me how their layer of tenderness had grown from
the ugliest possible wreckage.

For years they had fought about what Lee would do with his life. It was a
fight that had started back in chemistry class their junior year of high school.
At sixteen, Gracie fell in love with Lee and his brilliant mind. She wanted

him to go to Rice with her and become a chemist. But Lee hated pressure and didn't want to work in a lab the rest of his life. Instead of college, he went to trade school and became a plumber for a big franchise.

While Gracie was at Rice studying chemical engineering, she and Lee got married. After graduation, she landed a good job with an oil company, and in seven short years, she had been promoted to manager and had also given birth to three daughters. Gracie loved her job, and she worked past sunset most nights to close accounts and rack up big bonuses. Lee came home at four to watch TV. Yes, he made dinner every night, and yes, he helped the girls with their homework, but Gracie hated that he had no ambition, that he was wasting his talents on plumbing.

Sometimes, she was sarcastic about him not working more. Sometimes, she tried to understand him. Mostly, she stopped saying much to Lee. She masked her disappointment by spending even more time at her own job.

A man who worked sixty hours a week to reach his potential became Gracie's forbidden fruit. Over the next couple of months, Gracie spent more time with another manager at her company, Patrick.

He was also a type-A driver with aggressive goals. They became the dynamic duo, the ones who always closed the biggest accounts. Over business lunches and on sales trips, Gracie told Patrick stories about how Lee was wasting his life.

Patrick liked solving problems. Hearing Gracie's expectations for her husband sketched out a goal for him. In hindsight, Gracie can now see these were the ingredients for an affair; she felt entitled to have a husband who worked as hard as she did, and Patrick loved her depending on him. This pride and lust eventually led to them having drunken sex on a business trip.

Gracie said that for the next few months, when she and Patrick were sleeping together, she always felt wired, like she was downing Red Bulls all day. Plans and secrets were always pinging in her brain, and she couldn't really concentrate on anything. The sex on company trips and in parking garages made her both scared and jittery. Over thirteen weeks—nearly one hundred nights—she couldn't recall one night when she slept well.

Then, one Saturday morning, Lee discovered an email from Patrick with raunchy details about their last trip together. Suddenly, what he had suspected and feared was staring him in the face. Lee cried; Gracie cried. He told her she was selfish and would get exactly what she deserved. Then he moved his things into a hotel.

Over the next couple of weeks, Gracie spent every evening at Lee's hotel and confessed the truth about all the lies she had been living. Lee said things to her she never thought he could. She apologized in every way she knew how. Then, in the hardest moment of her life, Gracie had to tell their three daughters what she had done. She said she still loved their dad and would do anything to get him to move back.

Gracie left her job, cut off all contact with Patrick, and promised Lee she would change completely. Even now, as she shared this story over our lunch, she sobbed, remembering how terrified she had been. She said that this self-disgust would probably always be part of her. She still couldn't really forgive herself.

But Lee did forgive her, and he did decide to give their marriage a second chance. They called their pastor. They wanted to figure out what had gone wrong, and they needed help.

They discovered it had been pride that had almost ruined their marriage. Slowly, over millions of tiny, prideful moments, Gracie had convinced herself she deserved More, and More had become Patrick.

Lee's pride also hurt them. He liked to be the guy with the ideas—especially about his life. He rejected most of Gracie's plans just because he hadn't thought of them himself. He had felt stuck, but he didn't want her telling him what he should do. So he had done nothing.

Gracie shared her story with me as a cautionary tale. Pride causes so many sins in marriage. An affair, yes. But also so much more: trying to control each other, nagging, silent treatments, and screaming Friday-night fights. All that self-righteousness was part of their lives way before the affair actually happened.

Maybe Gracie's story scares you like it scared me. Because I know that pride; I see it every time I look in the mirror. I know how it feels to pout and manipulate and to pressure my husband into what I think he should do.

Maybe you can also see the little kernels of pride threatening to burst in your own marriage. You deserve to have your husband clean up his dirty clothes. You deserve a husband who will take you out on real dates. You deserve better—and better is a man who does exactly what you want.

This self-righteousness is like stinky garbage that buries the layers of intimacy in your marriage. You want more closeness with your husband, but it's lost in the fights over who's right and who's in control.

Jesus says the humbleness and intimacy are best. He says the poor in spirit, the meek, and the merciful are the blessed ones.

Self-righteousness has no place in your love story. Your marriage *can* be covered in the love of Christ. Start by wrapping your arms around your husband, and by telling him you're sorry for whatever's between you. Trust that both of your souls are way more elastic than you believe they are. Trust that the Holy Spirit will change your heart to be more pure, more peaceful, more giving.

Follow Jesus' example and His grace right to that place of humbleness, of sacrificial love. Burrow into the sweet spot in your marriage where pride and control have no place, and where God's meekness and mercy rule your hearts. These are the blessings God gives us through Jesus' sacrifice. Let's enjoy these gifts.

YOUR STORY/GOD'S STORY

1. We all struggle with pride. We all fall into the same sin Eve fell into when she believed she was entitled and chose independence from God. Talk about how the sins of entitlement and pride in your marriage can lead to an affair.

2. Read Genesis 2:22–24 and take a closer look at your identity in your marriage. God tells you that you are one flesh with this man. Is this also how you see your relationship with your husband? Is there room for pride in God's definition of marriage?

3. Read Luke 17:3–4 and Jesus' teaching about forgiveness. Pride convinces you it's a great idea to hold everything your husband has done wrong against him. Pride tells you, "If you forgive, you're not protecting yourself!" But God is clear that He wants you to stay married throughout your earthly life. And that's a really long time to keep reminding your husband about the New Year's Eve when he drank too much. Where do you need the Holy Spirit to change your heart on this?

4. In 2 Samuel 11, we see the story of how David (who had killed a *giant*) let the giant of entitlement rule in his life. David believed he deserved Bathsheba, and their adultery led to death, spiritual destruction, and generations of pain (2 Samuel 16:20–23; 1 Kings 1:11–31). Read David's confession in Psalm 51:10–12. How did God transform David's heart (2 Samuel 12:14–21)?

5. Where is pride covering up intimacy in your marriage? Look at Luther's words in his explanation of the Sixth Commandment. Part of this commandment is that we should love and honor our spouses. How would more love and honor help rid your marriage of pride?

PRAY . . .

Father, You are the source of everything good in my life. Even though You've given me everything I need, I forget I'm Your child and look in other places for happiness and security. I rebel against You and hurt those I love. Lord, change my heart so I am humble, like Your Son, Jesus. In His redeeming name. Amen.

The Endorphins
Will Carry You

*"I will give you a new heart, and a new spirit I will put within you.
And I will remove the heart of stone from your flesh and give you
a heart of flesh."*

—God in Ezekiel 36:26

SUMMER WAS COMING, and I needed to lose some weight. During our busy
spring, I had gotten in the habit of grabbing fast food and skipping the gym.
Now our calendar was filling up with bathing-suit activities, and my bathing
suit looked like the cardboard part of toilet paper stretched over the roll.

A friend of mine had just bought an Apple Watch and insisted it was the
fitness jolt I needed. The watch woke her up every morning and pushed her to
get her miles in. In one month, she had lost six pounds. This is what I needed.

But an Apple Watch was hundreds of dollars, and Mike was cynical that
a fancy watch had anything to do with fitness. He has run fifteen marathons
and is a firm believer that the only gear anyone needs is a good pair of shoes.

Not me, I explained. If I wanted to turn my donut-shop habit into a morning-
run habit, I needed to engage my emotions. I told Mike the watch would be my
carrot. When I could run a 5K in under thirty minutes, I would buy the watch.
I signed up for a race a month away and vowed to run every day.

The first couple of weeks were ugly. My lungs burned when I tried to run a
mile, and I had to stop and walk. My thick thighs chafed against each other.
My calf muscles stayed so tight, I hobbled up the steps at night.

The 5K was getting closer, but I could still run only about two miles. To motivate me, Mike started getting up early and joining me on the trails. Running together has never worked for us. He chats, runs fast, and always chooses the long route home. He's like the Richard Simmons of running; I'm like the Chris Farley. I started to sleep in, and he let me.

And then I had a really bad day, and to feel better, I bought the Apple Watch. Mike was out of town, and I was breathtakingly lonely. Everything was overwhelming in the way it is when hormones are probably involved. I didn't care about commitments or running or the race. I just wanted to feel happier. In less time than it took to run a mile, ordering that watch had already lightened my mood.

I tried to run the next morning, but my right hamstring hurt too much. I stopped on the trails while other runners passed me so I could Google "hamstring pain." Websites said I had pulled it. That sounded serious.

This was actually good news. If I was injured, I didn't have to run the race. I knew I wouldn't beat thirty minutes, and I already had the watch, so I dropped out.

On the morning of the 5K, Mike asked me to go for a run with him. We hadn't talked much about the watch or the deal I had made with myself. I told him my hamstring hurt, and he pointed out it was probably just getting stronger.

We started on the trails, and this time, running was easier. My ab muscles didn't cramp. My legs were corded with strong tendons. My lungs slowly expanded instead of gulping air. Mike and I passed other runners.

Then, suddenly, my brain cleared, like after a good sneeze. The trees looked Technicolor green, and my skin pimpled with goose bumps. Mike could hardly keep up with me. I ran up hills faster than I would have believed my thick thighs could carry me. I stopped at the top of a hill to wait for Mike and glanced at my watch. I had run exactly 3.10 miles. A 5K.

After that first endorphin rush, I became a junkie, and I started running every morning. I lost weight, yes, but I also learned about the rewards from training: lots of energy, new muscles, better sleep, and those sweet endorphins. The watch had just been a sexy distraction from all this, from what I really wanted all along.

Runners who cross the finish line will tell you it's the muscles that carry you there, not the emotions. They will tell you that training for a race is challenging. You will feel like you can't go any farther and that running is way harder for you than for anyone else.

But none of this is true; running is not harder for you, and you can always go farther. If you've done the training, you have already built the muscles and endurance you need to get to the finish line. I didn't need to engage my emotions in running. I didn't need an Apple Watch. I needed to get out on the trails and put one foot in front of the other. I needed to stick with the commitment, even when it was hard.

This is just like marriage.

We talk about the love in marriage—about the *emotion*—way more than we talk about the training and work. But emotion plays tricks on you. Emotions tell you that marriage is harder for you than for anyone else. When marriage feels painful and hard, emotion tells you to go and find someone newer and more exciting, someone to make you happy. Emotion tells you to quit when marriage doesn't feel good.

God doesn't want you chasing emotions; He wants His training to change you. He wants to turn your flabby self-centeredness into rock-hard muscles of service. He wants to turn your weak, prideful heart into your strongest organ of generosity and compassion.

Do the hard training in His Word because with that training come the exact rewards you want. Through serving your husband, you learn to serve God. Through humbleness, your heart expands to include people who need grace. Through the true forgiveness you show your husband, you learn to forgive yourself. These are the strong muscles that carry you.

But these muscles can take you only so far. Pretty soon, when you least expect it and when you need it the very most, the Holy Spirit gives you the spiritual endorphins. These moments of God's grace really carry you through the hard seasons.

And in these miracle moments, you will realize your own weakness.

More important, you see the Technicolor love of your Savior, the love that is all over your marriage.

YOUR STORY/GOD'S STORY

1. Are you a sprinter, someone with short bursts of energy and emotion, or a long-distance runner, a person who tackles life with slow, steady commitment? What challenges and benefits do you see in both personalities? How does each look in a marriage?

2. Two-thirds of those spouses who reported being in an unhappy marriage changed their answer a decade later to say their marriage was now happy. Talk about the implications of this research and how you've found this to be true. Have you experienced spiritual endorphins in marriage? How has God carried you through a hard time, only to give you a season of euphoria? Tell your story.

3. Read 2 Corinthians 5:17 and talk about how this relates to marriage. What does it mean to live as a new creation? What does it mean in marriage?

4. God blesses marriages with sex, commitment, family, real chances to learn trust, Christ's forgiveness, and opportunities for service. Talk about how these are the fundamental blessings of life. Why does God distribute them through marriage?

5. When Luther explains this commandment, he says that loving and honoring God means also loving and honoring your husband. How do you know that loving and honoring your husband will also honor God?

PRAY . . .

Father, thank You for loving me completely every single day of my life. Help me to love more like You do. Help me to learn from You so I can show grace in my most important relationships. Help me to love like Jesus, who died to save my soul. In His redeeming name. Amen.

Depressing Weddings

*Love is patient and kind; love does not envy or boast; it is not arrogant
or rude. It does not insist on its own way; it is not irritable or resentful;
it does not rejoice at wrongdoing, but rejoices with the truth. Love bears
all things, believes all things, hopes all things, endures all things.*

—Paul in 1 Corinthians 13:4–7

LAST WEEK OUR FAMILY WENT TO A WEDDING that was so beautiful and so
fun that I left feeling a little better about marriage. It was at a botanical garden, right in the middle of Houston's old warehouse district. Freeways, exhaust, and trash circled the high brick wall that protected the garden. Hidden
right behind that wall were fields of white, pink, and violet flowers.

The gardens were delicate and stunning. Before our family sat down, I took
pictures of the kids next to a little field of wide, white gardenias. The other
guests were also pulling out their phones to snap pictures, all of us captivated
by this chapel of flowers. The tone was set for an extraordinary evening.

Both the bride and groom came from Houston elite. Every detail—from
the strings of twinkling lights in the starry sky to the exact shade of cream rose
in the groom's boutonnière—was magazine perfect. By the time the willowy
blond bride said "I do" to her square-shouldered husband, I had fallen in love
with their wedding.

The band played the right mix of golden slow songs and timeless boogie-
down favorites. Our whole family danced until we were sweaty and had totally
forgotten our shoes and self-consciousness on the side of the dance floor.
When we left—our arms filled with the band's CD, chocolate in the shape
of the couple's monogram, and little wooden toys for the kids—we all felt in-

spired. Catie and Elisabeth were planning their own weddings, and the boys wanted to start a band.

As I fell asleep that night, my mind replayed footage from the evening. This wedding was more than just a chance to teach our kids line dances; it had been the reminder I had been looking for that happy marriages still happen.

During the past few years, weddings had started to seem a little depressing to me. More and more of our friends were divorcing, and among them was an older couple we admired. Could any marriage really be happy?

In the midst of those divorces, that wedding stuck out as hopeful, like those gardenias in the middle of the exhaust. Weddings were still beautiful, and marriages could still last. This lovely couple, with their heartfelt ceremony and hope, already seemed halfway to their fiftieth wedding anniversary.

Statistics would probably agree that this couple had some real advantages that would make them less likely to divorce. They were starting out without the usual strains: they had no money problems, they had dedicated parents who supported them, neither the bride nor groom had been married before, and they both love God. According to a therapist's checklist, the perfectly placed fondant on the couple's "love reigns forever" cupcakes didn't lie. Only death could part a couple with so much going for them, right?

But this kind of thinking leaves marriage entirely up to human effort. And if marriage depends on human effort, it is hopeless. What about our friends who were getting a divorce? They also had everything going for them. They had tried their hardest. What had happened?

I don't know exactly what happened with the couples getting divorced, but I can only guess their marriages followed the same trajectory my son's remote-controlled helicopter does. Straight up, apparent soaring success, then floundering, and *BAM!* Crash landing!

For many couples, the floundering begins after the first few years, when you realize you have married the most selfish person on the planet. He doesn't listen to your stories or appreciate your dinners or come home right after work. How could you not have noticed this before? This man is more self-centered than a toddler with a fever.

Unfortunately, he's probably realizing this same thing about you.

Over the next few years, you are sad to realize that your husband will not supply what you thought he would. He is not going to be able to give you your identity or your security or even your happiness.

This is where most marriages flounder, where the helicopter starts circling. You tell yourself you made a mistake. Time to find someone who can fill you up. Maybe your old boyfriend who just sent you a Facebook message . . . he was always so good at listening . . .

But God tells you to stop right there. He tells us that another person cannot really give you your identity or your security. The old boyfriend will disappoint you, just as your husband has already disappointed you.

God says that life is about serving Him and others. Your marriage is not a lifelong course in teaching your husband to care for you and your idiosyncrasies. Marriage is, actually, the exact opposite. It's a lifelong commitment to losing your selfishness and learning true service.

We don't have to be cynical about marriage because it's not a celebration of our human love; it's a celebration of what God will do in our lives. He commands us to a life of forever love, but He also equips us for that life.

So, yes, we can celebrate at weddings. We don't have to worry about how hard the marriage will be. Instead, we can trust how incredible God's love and lessons of Jesus' forgiveness will be.

Let's dance until we're sweaty, friends. Marriage is a miracle.

YOUR STORY/GOD'S STORY

1. We all can become cynical about marriage. Who in your circle of friends or in your family is divorced? How have these divorces changed your hope for marriage? Tell these stories. Has adultery played a part in all of them?

2. If you've been divorced, talk about that experience. What does it feel like to untangle your life from a person you expected to love forever (Mark 10:9)? What did you learn about what God wants for marriage?

3. Read John 8:1–11. What else do we learn about adultery here? What is at the heart of every commandment, including this one?

4. Read Matthew 19:4–6. God wants a husband and wife to become one flesh in earthly marriage. Talk about how this makes your husband your most intimate partner in Christ. How does melting together into one flesh make you work together so both of you change to know, imitate, serve, and worship God as one flesh?

5. The explanation of this commandment talks about how important our words and deeds are in marriage. Think about how you treat your husband and how he treats you. What would more of God's love look like in your marriage going forward?

PRAY . . .

Father, Your love is so powerful, so complete, so transforming, it gives me everything I need. Help me to share this love with my husband. Help me to sacrifice to honor and love Him. Help me to follow Jesus' example of total love and surrender. In His redeeming name. Amen.

A Letter to My Eleven-Year-Old Daughter

Flee from sexual immorality. Every other sin a person commits is outside the body, but the sexually immoral person sins against his own body. Or do you not know that your body is a temple of the Holy Spirit within you, whom you have from God? You are not your own, for you were bought with a price. So glorify God in your body.

—Paul in 1 Corinthians 6:18–20

DEAR CATIE,

I really don't want to write this letter to you. It's awkward and hard to discuss sex with you. It's especially awkward to talk about the idea of you ever having sex.

I happen to be writing this as you're just beginning middle school. You are starting this season understanding sex as only biological. But this will soon change. Your peers, the media, and even your own body are about to try to convince you that sex is the biggest deal in the world.

Then, as you get even older and go to high school, sex will be about the only thing anyone seems to talk about. Some days, you'll feel like every conversation is about sex. Who's had sex and who hasn't had sex? Did she have sex with him, and are they planning to have sex anytime soon? What happened when they had sex, and what are they going to do now? You'll look at strangers in the mall and wonder if every person is thinking about sex all the time.

And maybe some of them are—sort of. Our bodies are made up of different appetites (hunger, thirst, rest, sex). An appetite for sex rules some people. They seem to think about it, indulge in it, and talk about it all the time. When they tell us sex is the most important part of life, it feels true to them. It does start to feel true for all of us.

It's not the truth, though. Sex is a very good thing, a very wonderful part of marriage, but it should not and cannot be the focus of your life. God gave us lots of different relationships, lots of different interests, lots of different gifts and experiences, lots of incredible ways to relate to boys and to one another. Believing sex is the only one that matters doesn't sound quite right, does it?

It isn't right, honey.

Imagine your life was only a quest to find the very best meal. Every single minute of every single day, you looked only at pictures of bacon and chocolate cake. You only talked and thought about finding the creamiest frosting and coldest glass of fresh milk. Your life would be out of order—and kind of sad. Eating is for calories, not obsession.

Sex also has a really specific purpose. It's not like our other appetites that we fill up every time we need to. God gave sex as the glue for your future marriage. Sex is for the specific job of melding your soul to your husband's soul. Because sex is powerful, in God's supernatural way, it's meant to be celebrated with a lifelong commitment attached to it.

In a world like ours, where sex is everywhere, the idea that you should have sex with only one person in your whole life will sound crazy, old-fashioned, and even a little stupid. But saving sex for your husband is truly what's best for you, Catie.

I know you're smart enough to see the discrepancy here: if saving sex for marriage is such a good decision, why doesn't anyone else seem to be doing that? You will feel alone, and you'll start to believe that you're missing out by not having sex before you're married.

And everyone will tell you exactly that. But that's a lie that's usually told by people who will gain a lot from you believing it. Your friends who have sex with their boyfriends will feel the incredible connection it provides (the connection meant for marriage). They will also feel the weight and guilt that goes with that connection. They will want you to sleep with your boyfriend because if absolutely everyone does this, they'll feel better about it.

A boy who wants to have sex with you might tell you sex is a huge deal to him. Maybe he's not lying. Maybe it's a huge deal because he's living in the world of sexual obsession and his cravings are following that. Maybe it's a huge deal because he really loves you. But sex is a lifetime commitment, and a boyfriend isn't. This is a really important distinction.

The media and the world will also tell you, over and over again, that having sex is empowering. But this is also a lie. Movies, TV shows, and books will promise you that sex makes you more normal, more mature, and more loved. But again, these are just wrong labels for that powerful connection you feel with sex. God made the connection so strong because He wants it to seal marriages together forever.

During puberty, no one talks much about saving sex for marriage because that belief doesn't seem to benefit anyone right now. But this is where you want to stand up for yourself and your husband. Your choice now—the choice of a pure marriage, of a bond with the person you really will love more than anyone else—matters for the rest of your life.

This is the really good news: your heavenly Father—your Creator—loves you so much, He wants the very best for you. And He loved you so much that He sent His Son to die for you. He loves you so much that He wants you to follow His plan for marriage.

Thank you for reading this, sweetheart. This is important.

I LOVE YOU,
MOM

YOUR STORY/GOD'S STORY

1. Share your own advice about sex before marriage. If you could go back to the start of middle school, what would you tell yourself?

2. Christians define premarital sex as adultery, and this includes living together. Talk about what our culture teaches about this. What's the problem?

3. Read Matthew 1:18–22, the most famous story in the Bible, the story of a young girl who was accused of premarital sex. How did Joseph react when he thought his fiancée had committed adultery? What was the potential punishment for Mary (see John 8:4–5)? Talk about how society's view toward premarital sex has changed and what medical advancements contributed to this change. What damage is still done when teens have sex?

4. Consider why God gives us choice when it comes to premarital sex. What if a couple were only capable of sex *after* they were married? Does giving humans the power to choose to wait for marriage make the bond even more special?

5. In the explanation of this commandment, Luther teaches that not committing adultery means a lifetime of purity. Talk about how not having premarital sex when you're younger shows love and honor to your husband. How can you teach this message to the next generation?

PRAY . . .

Lord, You always want to protect my body and soul. Help me to follow Your command of purity. Keep my thoughts and body clean. Change my heart to not lust but to honor You. Thank You for the example of Jesus, who modeled a pure and perfect life. In His redeeming name. Amen.

Don't Steal

"You shall not steal."

—God in Exodus 20:15

"Do not lay up for yourselves treasures on earth, where moth and rust destroy and where thieves break in and steal, but lay up for yourselves treasures in heaven, where neither moth nor rust destroys and where thieves do not break in and steal. For where your treasure is, there your heart will be also."

—Jesus in Matthew 6:19–21

THE KIDS' CHRISTMAS GIFTS had been disappearing one by one. We had a thief living in our house, and no one was confessing.

The whole family searched when Sam couldn't find the games for his Nintendo DS. Then we looked everywhere for Elisabeth's favorite elephant, Winks. When Catie's Kindle went missing, we organized a Saturday-morning search party for the stolen goods. Nate wasn't missing anything, but I figured he was too young to realize it if he was. We interrogated the kids over and over. No one had any leads.

Then Nate cleaned his room, and I helped him pull the dirty socks and library books from under his bed. And there, in a dark corner, was the treasure trove of stolen goods.

Mike and I freaked out. "WHY ARE YOU STEALING? WHY DID YOU LIE ABOUT STEALING? YOU CANNOT TAKE WHAT'S NOT YOURS!"

Nate explained he knew all that, but that he *had* to take things because we never gave him anything good.

I'm sure the youngest in every family believes this. The big kids get all the cool stuff. When your older brother is unwrapping a Mega Super Soaker, the Legos you're opening don't have the same pizzazz.

Mike and I told Nate that Sam had also gotten Legos at his age and that he should be satisfied with his gifts. Nate still didn't get the message. A month later, Sam's new Jedi costume was missing. We checked the dark corner under Nate's bed, and there it was.

Stealing is a sin that we all struggle with throughout life. You and I are not stealing Super Soakers from one another, but we do find all kinds of shady ways to get a little more. Employees steal billions of dollars from their companies every year by saying they work more than they actually do. Tax fraud is more of a problem than ever before. Our email accounts, cell phones, and credit cards all need protection against theft. We live in a culture where stealing is not just a crime and not just a sin—it's expected.

But God tells us that stealing is a double-whammy sin. It hurts your neighbor when you take her gifts. It hurts you when you believe in your greed that more things will satisfy you.

Our treasures are in heaven, not here. Our clothes, bank accounts, and houses will eventually fall apart—but not our eternal gifts, not love, true peace, and deep joy. These are the better treasures, Jesus said. These are the treasures that are ours through His sacrifice.

These are the treasures we can't stockpile or steal—and these are the gifts we really need.

THOUGHTS ABOUT THIS COMMANDMENT

1. Luther says the Seventh Commandment means "We should fear and love God so that we do not take our neighbor's money or possessions, or get them in any dishonest way, but help him to improve and protect his possessions and income." Doesn't this scheming sound so . . . so familiar to us today? Think about your week, your month, your year. When has someone taken your money or property or scammed you with a bad product or deal? Now, a harder question: have you done this to anyone else?

2. What about the second part of the explanation: "but help him to improve and protect his possessions and income"? Talk about how rare this kind of attitude is in today's world. Do you know anyone who helps other people improve and protect their businesses? What's the deeper command here? Look at John 15:12.

Shopping & Prozac

"How difficult it is for those who have wealth to enter the kingdom of God! For it is easier for a camel to go through the eye of a needle than for a rich person to enter the kingdom of God."
Those who heard it said, "Then who can be saved?"
But [Jesus] said, "What is impossible with man is possible with God."

—Jesus in Luke 18:24–27

GROWING UP, MY FAMILY FELL closer to the side of financial insecurity than the side of financial comfort. We were late for school because our old van would stall. My parents fought about hot checks and mortgage payments. New clothes were not in the budget, so we waited for hand-me-downs from friends at church.

I can remember the afternoon when I realized we were probably poor. My mom was in the grocery store while my brother and I waited in our old van. My parents were worried about paying bills, and my brother and I were trying to figure out a way we could help. Maybe we could combine our piggy banks with the extra quarters on Dad's dresser. Maybe I could get a job when I turned seven.

My insecurity about money grew over the next few years. As I realized other families didn't worry about money like ours did, I learned to lie. I didn't want anyone to know my mom had to stretch fifty dollars from my grandpa to buy us Christmas, so I lied that I had gotten records and makeup.

I began to see our family as the one who couldn't afford what the rest of the world could. Everything wrong with us was because we didn't have enough money. Just like a sick woman pins all her dreams on the day she can get out of bed, a poor girl pins her hope on the day she can buy whatever she wants.

At age 14, I lied about my age to get my first job bringing schnitzels to tourists at a German restaurant. That first paycheck felt like my winning lottery ticket.

I went straight to the mall and spent every penny on Bass shoes and fancy overalls from the Gap. I felt so powerful, I might as well have had a Black American Express. The weight of those shopping bags in my hands was like a shot of Prozac.

In high school, I wanted more and more new things, but I didn't have enough money. So I shoplifted. I'm so ashamed to remember these scenes: me crouched in dressing rooms, ripping price tags off with my teeth; me smuggling shorts out in my purse, holding my breath as I walked under the security sensors. I don't know why other kids shoplift, but I know why I did—because I wanted new stuff that I didn't have enough money to buy.

Every weekend, my friends and I drove to Baybrook Mall to sneak outfits out of The Limited, Macy's, and Benetton. The risk of getting arrested was nothing compared with having new things. We *needed* this stuff: CDs, giant hoop earrings, white denim miniskirts, and more nail polish than we could use in three decades.

Three decades later, as I write this, I'm embarrassed and guilty. What kind of rotten selfishness made me keep doing what I knew was wrong, over and over, every weekend?

But if I'm being honest, I haven't changed. Not really. I may not be smuggling miniskirts out of Benetton, but my rotten greed is still my quicksand. The more money and stuff I get, the more I want. Over the past eighteen years, God has given Mike and me enough money to make my six-year-old self feel secure. I have bought all the clothes and nail polish that high school girl could ever want. We are buried in stuff, but I want more, more, more.

I'm not alone in this. My friends, our neighbors, and the other moms at our kids' school are shopping every day too. They spend their weekends looking for better cars. We lie awake at night, strategizing how we can save more money for retirement and our kids' college. We all need more, and we will do what we have to do so we can get it.

None of us is running Ponzi schemes, but maybe we have stories about using dishonest tax loopholes, about billing clients without doing the work, or about accepting what no one could ever realize isn't ours.

Stealing isn't a hand issue; it's a heart issue. New stuff still works like Prozac, and big paychecks still feel like winning lottery tickets. Our minds have learned that money doesn't buy happiness, but our hearts aren't listening—they're looking for ways to earn a bigger bonus.

God didn't intend for me to see money as my savior when I was an insecure little girl, and He doesn't intend us to see it like that now. We can't change this greed on our own. We can only trust that God will keep teaching us the truth about greed in whatever way makes the most sense to each one of us.

So, this is my prayer: God, please keep showing us that our identities are in You, not in our status as rich or poor. Correct us when we believe the lie that more stuff and more money will give us more security. Let us see the gifts You've already given us through Jesus, our Savior. Fill each one of us with the security we need. Keep us coming back to You.

In the name of Christ, who has already claimed us as His.

Amen.

YOUR STORY/GOD'S STORY

1. Greed is at the core of every one of our hearts. Fear tells us we need more, and stealing is fear in action. Think of your story. When have you let greed rule your heart, and how has God shown you that greed is a lie?

2. Jesus had a lot to say about greed. A lot of His teaching was about money. Why do you think Jesus talked about finances so much?

3. Talk about the wisdom you've learned from 1 Timothy 6:6–10. What harm does the love of money cause? How does God protect us against loving money?

4. Read Luke 16:10–13. Talk about the connection Jesus makes between serving money as your god and your trustworthiness. What does this tell you about greed and about someone who serves money as her god? Can you trust a person like this?

5. What does it mean to not steal? It means realizing God gave gifts to

your neighbors that He wants them to keep. Every time we take some-
thing that isn't ours, we take the blessing God gave to that person.
Because we love God, we don't take our neighbor's money or property.
Is there a place in your life where you're lusting for someone else's gifts?
How can this change?

PRAY . . .

Heavenly Father, thank You for the perfect gifts You give me and my
family. Lord, forgive me when I believe that more things will make
me happier. Make my heart content, Father, in what You have blessed
me with today. Turn my eyes to Jesus and His sacrifice so I can better
understand Your transforming love. In His redeeming name. Amen.

Sisters & Stealing

Someone in the crowd said to Him, "Teacher, tell my brother to divide the
inheritance with me."
But He said to him, "Man, who made Me a judge or arbitrator over
you?" And He said to them, "Take care, and be on your guard against
all covetousness, for one's life does not consist in the abundance of his
possessions."

—Jesus in Luke 12:13–15

My friend Emma grew up in a close-knit Christian family on a small
working farm here in Katy, Texas. Her family valued loyalty and hard work
more than anything else. They took care of one another. After college at Texas
A&M, Emma and her husband moved back to Katy to begin their family.

In the years Emma had been gone, the city had grown from a dusty farm
town into one crowded with new malls, Thai restaurants, six thousand frozen
yogurt places, and brand-new schools. Emma's parents still had their property
in the middle of town, and her dad still farmed—right until the day he found
out he had brain cancer, the kind that spread quickly and that surgery couldn't
help.

At the time, Emma's sister lived in California and was going through an
ugly divorce. She and her husband were fighting over the kids, and she was
able to come home only twice to visit her dad. Emma was alone to help her
folks. She spent most days at her parents' house, feeding animals and getting
groceries. She drove her dad to radiation appointments, slept at the hospital,
and made lasagna—her parents' favorite food—by the panful.

Emma's dad died that summer.

I met Emma in a book club that started a few weeks after her dad's funeral. She told the group the story of losing him. She wanted to be finished with this sad season so she could get back to life with her husband and kids.

Emma's next season proved to be even sadder. Her mom started forgetting everything: if she had fed the dogs, where she kept the checkbook, and how to drive to Emma's house. The doctors diagnosed Alzheimer's. Suddenly, Emma was right back where she had been, helping her mom with doctor's appointments and six prescriptions. Every month at book club, my friend looked a year older.

As Katy had grown, her family's twenty-acre farm had become valuable. Its prime location meant Emma's mom could sell it for over a million dollars, which they could really use for her care. Purging the house, finding a nursing home, and convincing her mom to move were all up to Emma.

Emma called her sister periodically to tell her what was happening, but the relationship was strained. Her sister was married again and had a new baby. Even when Emma moved their mom into an assisted-living facility, her sister couldn't come home. Emma felt alone in caring for her mom, and she was also so sick of her sister's busy new family. What about her first family, who needed her?

Long before, when their dad was diagnosed with cancer, Emma had become the sole power of attorney for her parents. She transferred money from their accounts to hers to pay for prescriptions, hospital bills, and groceries. She tried to keep the bills and accounts separate, but sickness and death aren't organized processes. She got in the habit of putting everything on her own credit card and then transferring money from her parents' account to pay the bill every few months.

When their mom broke her hip, Emma's sister came to visit. Her new family was stable now, and she planned to stay for two weeks. She asked Emma if she could see the accounts. She followed Emma around the house, asking her lots of questions. Why did Emma deposit money from the land deals into her own checking account? Couldn't she get a credit card in her mom's name? Was this really *all* the money?

In the fight Emma described as "horrible and awkward," Emma's sister accused her of stealing. The bills for their mom's care didn't add up to the tens of thousands of dollars missing from her account. Emma asked her sister how she would know how much it had cost to take care of their mom when she hadn't been there. Emma's sister wanted a CPA to review the accounts. Emma told her she had no right to question how she took care of their mom, and that it would be better if she went back to California.

Over the next couple of years, Emma's mom died, and the battle with her sister grew uglier. Her sister threatened to hire an attorney, and Emma had her number blocked on her cell phone. Emma could not imagine why her sister was being so hateful. Was this how she grieved? Had she always been this selfish? What about her family values? Where was her loyalty?

And then, as time passed, Emma started to think more about what had happened during those hard years. She missed her mom, her dad, and her sister—and only one of those was still alive. Now that some of the emotion had drained from that season, she wanted to find a way to reconnect.

Emma looked back at the accounts and realized she actually had been taking money from her parents' estate. On the credit card bills—bills paid from her parents' accounts—there was a family ski vacation, clothes for the kids, Christmas gifts, and lots of dinners out.

We talked about why she had used her parents' money to pay for that and why she hadn't realized it. This was obvious to Emma. She deserved it. She was working so hard, and the money was payment for that.

Watching Emma sort through her feelings about this was a little like watching someone go through childbirth. When your contractions are unbearable, the nurses tell you to focus on a stationary point, a small, still place in the room. When you're losing your mind with pain, staring at a single point helps your brain understand that the frantic pain is temporary.

When Emma rehashed all the ways her sister had let her down, she was frantic with resentment and bitterness. She could justify every penny she had taken. But when she focused on the quiet, still point of God's wisdom, she saw her own greed, and she knew she had been wrong.

Emma asked God to take away her frantic neediness and keep her eyes focused on Him. She asked her sister for forgiveness. She forgave herself for choosing what she knew wasn't totally honest.

Our lives as forgiven sinners are a constant battle between focusing on the frantic stress of this world and fixing our eyes on Jesus. It's a tension between believing our insatiable need for security and the still point of God's promise to provide.

God knows that we'll always choose the painful, frantic route, so He keeps working on our hearts. He keeps showing us Himself in His Word, in His Sacraments. He keeps inviting us to trust what He knows is best for us.

The grace and mercy, love and sacrifice of Jesus remain stable—now and forever more—as the focal point for our frantic hearts and minds.

YOUR STORY/GOD'S STORY

1. We steal when we believe we deserve something more than another person does. How does our pride fuel this lie? Where do you see this in your life?

2. We often take what's not ours because it feels like it won't hurt anyone else. Talk about a time you've believed this lie. Look at Mark 12:31. What part of God's command does this belief violate?

3. Read 2 Corinthians 4:16–18. Have you ever felt like the pain or greed or fear of this world could crush you, only to look up and see the still point of God's protection and grace? Tell your story about God's constant blessings in your life.

4. Read Luke 12:22–34. Here we go! Here we can see the promises of God versus the concerns of humans. God guarantees us love, protection, and constant, perfect care. What are we concerned about as humans? How does Jesus respond? What is Jesus' main point here?

5. In the explanation of the commandment, we see that God wants us to help our neighbors improve and protect their things. Is there someone who is in a vulnerable position right now and needs help protecting her investments (someone going through a nasty divorce, being taken advantage of in a scam, or experiencing identity theft)? Is there a way you could help?

PRAY . . .

Father God, You are the eternal, the constant, the everlasting one. Because of my sin, I often feel frantic and convinced I need more. Tune my heart to Your love, Lord, so I can rest in Your true peace. Thank You for sending Your Son so I can spend eternity with You. In His redeeming name. Amen.

Rise Up & Whine!

Let the thief no longer steal, but rather let him labor, doing honest work with his own hands, so that he may have something to share with anyone in need.

—Paul in Ephesians 4:28

OUR CHURCH'S PRESCHOOL wasn't looking too good. For decades, little muddy hands had smeared the walls. Teachers had stapled artwork in hallways and left little holes in every piece of the chipping paint. Classes doubled in size, but the classrooms stayed tiny. The wiring was archaic, and the fire marshal kept warning us the time was coming to shut down the school—or build a new one. No one in the congregation argued when the leadership team asked to raise $1 million for a new building.

I followed the discussions and voters meetings with detached interest—until our pastor called and asked me to serve as the communications director for the Rise Up and Build campaign. The position meant hours of work designing logos, writing letters, and creating newsletters.

Just as I was about to claim I was too busy, he read me the list of volunteers. Already committed was a woman whose young son had cancer, a man who had just lost his wife, and a couple with a baby due any day. I had no excuse. I knew I needed to help out.

I went to the Rise Up and Build meetings with all of the enthusiasm of an eleven-year-old at confirmation. I slouched in the back and scrolled Instagram on my phone. I figured everyone on the committee would also be cynical about the hours this campaign would take.

But no, they seemed excited. This new preschool would share Jesus with our city for decades to come! The building would be the place of kids' first memories, where some children first met Jesus. This is where kids would first learn to read!

Our pastor taught Bible studies about giving, and prayer teams met to pray for us to all understand the joy of giving. Every week a different person from the leadership team started the meeting by sharing his or her testimony. Each story had the same theme: we are giving to the preschool because we want to share what God has given us.

Clearly God was changing people through the Bible studies and prayers, but I shared zero of their enthusiasm. What was my problem? Was it because my kids were older and had gone to a different preschool? Was I burnt out from all the hours I spent creating those logos and newsletters? Was my small heart just too selfish to give to this ministry?

As Mike and I talked about our donation, I realized it was totally the last reason—my small heart. He would throw out a number, and I would justify why it was too much: we already gave money to the church; we needed to buy new kitchen appliances with that money; everyone else was giving so much, so why did we need to too?

Our congregation's excitement was at a fever pitch. Everyone was wearing rubber Rise Up and Build bracelets and bringing their commitment cards to church. Our congregation had dedicated more than $2 million, and we still had a month left in the campaign.

Two million dollars—I couldn't believe it! I started to listen more closely to the people's stories about giving. Most of them I had heard before: everything we have is on loan from God, and it feels so good to give. But a new idea was spreading among our friends, the idea that if you can support a ministry and choose not to, then you are stealing from God.

Was this true? Was not giving when I could stealing from God and His people?

Yes, maybe so. The bad news was that my problems with money went even deeper. I wanted to keep my money because of the power it gave me. I didn't want anyone telling me it belonged to someone else. Not even God.

In the end, our congregation gave over $3 million to the Rise Up and Build campaign. Mike and I did give to the campaign, but not as much as we could have. I don't know why my heart was never changed like our friends' hearts were.

But I do know that the Holy Spirit is still working on me. We are giving more than before. God keeps teaching me to trust Him. He's showing me He takes better care of me than I take of myself. He loves me more than I can understand. He's teaching me that the money I have isn't mine to begin with; it's His. He keeps saying, "Dear daughter, unclench your fists. Let Me be your first love. Trust Me."

Our church has started construction on our new preschool. None of us expected that our congregation could raise $3 million. Through those Bible studies and prayers, God changed so many hearts and called many families to live differently, to rise up and build in His name.

These new preschool classrooms will stand as testimonies of how God makes the impossible possible. But even more than that, the teachers in these classrooms will tell the kids about a God who loves them and will take care of them forever.

He is our heavenly Father, who sent His Son to claim each and every one of us as His children.

And that is the best testimony imaginable.

YOUR STORY/GOD'S STORY

1. Take an honest look at your own generosity. When it comes to giving to ministries, do you listen to God's call? If you've ever given more than you thought you could spare, talk about that experience. On the flip side, have you ever felt like you have not given, like you're stealing from God?

2. Sometimes, we look at stewardship as one act: tithing. Talk about how God's call for us to live a Christian life includes sharing all our gifts. Which of your gifts do you cheerfully share? Which ones do you struggle to share?

3. Read 2 Corinthians 9:7. God not only wants us to give, but He also wants us to give happily. How does this help us understand our relationship with Him and our relationship with money?

4. The Holy Spirit wants to transform our hearts from greediness. Look at the parable of the sower (Matthew 13:1–30), especially Matthew 13:22. Money and greed threaten to choke out the Word of God in our lives. But what does the Spirit do?

5. The explanation of this commandment is that we fear and love God, and because of this, we should not steal. Take this one step further. How could your love and gratitude for God's blessings help you to be more generous? Talk about what more joyful giving would look like in your life.

PRAY . . .

Heavenly Father, You created everything in this world. You sustain and manage every part of my life. Because I'm selfish, Lord, I believe my time, money, and talents belong to me. Help me to see that everything I have belongs to You, dear Father. Help me to give freely, just like You freely gave Your Son. In His redeeming name. Amen.

House Hunters

Trust in the LORD with all your heart, and do not lean on your own understanding.
In all your ways acknowledge Him, and He will make straight your paths.
Be not wise in your own eyes; fear the LORD, and turn away from evil.
It will be healing to your flesh and refreshment to your bones.

—Solomon in Proverbs 3:5–8

LOOKING FOR A NEW HOUSE started out as a lot of fun. It was like a reality show where we got to peek into other people's closets and imagine how our life would fit into their living rooms. Even though our kids (one-year-old twins and a three-year-old at the time) would have rather spent their Saturdays watching *Mickey Mouse Clubhouse*, we took them house hunting because we desperately needed more space.

For twenty straight Saturdays, we met our real estate agent to look for our forever home, preferably one with a big backyard, in a nice neighborhood, with lots of neighbor kids and parks and good schools. Yes, our list of must-haves was long, but we planned to persevere until we found our house.

We had saved for several years, squirreling away money in an Ameritrade account and watching our savings grow every year. Unfortunately, this was in 2008, and the stock market was about to crash. We didn't know that yet.

Our real estate agent suggested we get our own house on the market, just in case that sale took a long time. We purged our closets, rented a third storage unit to hold our clutter, and put a For Sale sign in the yard.

Our house sold immediately. The first hour of the first day, a family made us an offer we couldn't refuse. They were moving from England, and the ship delivering their belongings would arrive in a month. Could we pack everything and be out in a month? Would we be able to find a new house in time? Our real estate agent advised us to take the offer. We prayed this would all work out. Then we clenched our eyes shut, signed the papers, and tried not to freak out.

Thirty days until we're homeless. GO!

The next month was crazy. We looked at houses every day, whittling down our list of must-haves more and more. We made lowball offers on homes we couldn't afford. We offered more than the asking price on houses we wanted, writing in the contract that the occupants had to be out in three weeks. When neither of those worked, we made offers on houses we thought we might get but didn't really like.

Then the stock market crashed. For two days, every time we checked our Ameritrade account, the balance had fallen. Every analyst and financial adviser gave the same advice: Don't panic and don't sell! The market will bounce back!

But we had to sell; we needed the money *now* to buy a house. The day we cashed in everything was also the day the stock market hit a thirty-year low. Our price range was suddenly cut in half, and we had to start looking at smaller houses. The only thing disappearing faster than our money was our time. We had three weeks before the English family moved in, and we had no place to go.

We made an offer on a wonky house that neither of us liked, just because it was vacant. The sellers accepted our offer, and I cried in frustration. Three months before, we wouldn't have given this house a second look; now, it was our new home.

We liked the quiet neighborhood with parks and good schools, but the house was weird—very sleek and sterile, with a tiny backyard. It felt like a hospital, all white tile and long, wide hallways. We wanted the houses we had looked at last year and had been too picky to buy. We wanted our stock account to be what it had been last month. We wanted more time.

We went to our real estate agent and told her this all felt so wrong. Was there *anything* we could do? Break the contract with the family moving into our house? Invent some problem with the buyers' funding and tell them they couldn't have our house? Make an offer on one of the houses we really wanted, one of them that we couldn't afford, and then scrounge for more money? We looked her straight in the eye and told her we were desperate.

We were ready to do whatever dishonest move she suggested. If she'd said we needed to lie or cheat, we would have done it. We felt penned in, like a scared dog that bites when it's trapped. The stock market had cheated us, and we were ready to cheat someone else. The mortgage industry was filled with problems and lies, right? What were the loopholes?

Even though our real estate agent was a tough, savvy woman, she wasn't helping us out on this one. "This is how life goes sometimes. Don't panic. Trust."

Trust who? God? We had trusted God when we had twice the money. We had trusted God when we had dozens of options. We had trusted God when we thought we would have months to move. Trusting God had gotten us in the tightest corner of our lives.

We had one day left in our buying option period, and Mike was looking at houses on the Internet. The unstable economy meant more and more were for sale every day.

"Hey! Look at this!" He pointed to an image on the screen. "This is our house."

And there it was. On the next street over from the house we were buying, in the neighborhood we loved, a new house had just come on the market.

This house was gorgeous, with a huge front porch, a big backyard, enough bedrooms for all our kids, attic space converted into an enormous playroom, and right around the corner from the park. This was *our* house—we knew it in that way you know you've just met the person you'll marry.

We called our real estate agent. She could meet us at the house in twenty minutes.

Tears were in my eyes as we walked through every room. This house had every single one of our must-haves from the list we had made two years ago. This house even had weird things we loved, like a formal dining room that fit our table and an art niche for our favorite painting. And the price was right.

With shaking hands, we wrote an offer. We had the exact amount for the down payment from selling our stocks. The sellers, who had also been hit hard by the financial crisis, accepted our offer. They could move out fast. With just hours left in our option period, we canceled the other contract.

This was from God. He had sifted our money and time and options down to just this one, just the house, the one meant for us. That day in our Realtor's office, when we were ready to beg, borrow, or steal to get what we wanted, God didn't let any of that happen. He wanted us to understand who was taking care of our family. This was our Gideon moment.

In the story of Gideon, God sifted his troops down to almost nothing so Gideon would see God was the one taking care of him. Gideon shouldn't have won the battle against the Midianites, and on his own, he wouldn't have. But God made it happen in His perfect timing.

When we had no time and little money, we found our dream house, the one we had been looking for all along. The timing of this made no sense. This wasn't luck. This was God.

God made it rain on the hottest day of our drought. He provided in such a dramatic, supernatural way, we couldn't point to ourselves to take the credit. We didn't need to steal or scheme to get the house we wanted; God was doing something bigger here.

Jesus said, "In My Father's house are many rooms. If it were not so, would I have told you that I go to prepare a place for you?" (John 14:2). The same God who provided Jesus the sacrifice for me, who provides heaven for me, gave me exactly the right house.

God had taken care of our family the whole time. Because of this, we could trust that He would take care of us forever.

YOUR STORY/GOD'S STORY

1. Every believer has a story about a time when God took miraculous care of her—when He cared for her in such a dramatic way that she knew it was her Father. What's your story about a time God took dramatic care of you?

2. So often, we take our blessings for granted, assuming we are entitled to have them. What does entitlement make you do? What is something you feel like you deserve? How does this change the way you see your blessings? Do your gifts (children, money, time, friends) feel like something you've earned?

3. Read about Gideon in Judges 7. The most interesting part of Gideon's story is how he dealt with the pressures from the world. His people desperately needed to win this battle, and Gideon's troops were relying on him to battle like they thought he should. But God had Gideon lead the battle in unconventional ways that no human commander would have chosen for his troops. What expectations are you facing right now? How are you reacting?

4. Read 1 Timothy 6:7 and consider this wisdom: "You never see a U-Haul behind a hearse." What treasures is God storing for you in heaven? How is the Holy Spirit helping you see this?

5. When we're scared, we look for shady deals that can help us get more stuff. Have you ever used the world's faulty economy to your advantage to get more? Is there a place in your life right now where you're looking for deals or scams to help you get ahead? How does this attitude hurt your relationship with God?

PRAY . . .

Lord, You give me Your perfect gifts at exactly the perfect time. In my sin, I believe in myself and in my own abilities. Clear the pride from my eyes, Father, and transform my heart to trust You. Thank You for sending Your Son at the fullness of time to save us from our sin. In His redeeming name. Amen.

Don't Bear False Witness against Your Neighbor

"You shall not bear false witness against your neighbor."

—God in Exodus 20:16

"Out of the abundance of the heart the mouth speaks. The good person out of his good treasure brings forth good, and the evil person out of his evil treasure brings forth evil. I tell you, on the day of judgment people will give account for every careless word they speak, for by your words you will be justified, and by your words you will be condemned."

—Jesus in Matthew 12:34–37

STORIES ARE THE OXYGEN AND CARBON DIOXIDE OF OUR SOULS. We breathe stories in to understand one another and ourselves. We breathe stories out to vent, to verbally process, and to make a point. Seriously, I just came from lunch with a group of women, and we were all interrupting one another with our stories. Our table sounded like a therapy session: stories about fear, joy, anger, hurt. No deep breaths, just the sharing and learning and rat-a-tat stories.

One friend said she was afraid her daughter had a learning disability. She shared how her third grader's homework takes two aggravating hours, and she's still making Ds. A dear friend complained how her husband spends money. She told a story about him walking into the dealership and buying a new Ford F-150. Another woman told how angry she is at her neighbor who didn't invite her family to a block party.

Like Jesus said in Matthew 12, our mouths speak from the abundance living in our hearts. Sometimes our hearts are abundant with love, sometimes they're abundant with confusion—but lots of times our hearts are abundant with jealousy, anger, and nastiness.

It's when our hearts are nasty that our stories become weapons. We tell stories to show we're victims. We tell stories to convert people to our opinions—especially our opinions about the people we don't like. We tell stories to make people like us more than they like anyone else.

God tells us not to do this. Don't reduce another person down to your narrative. God is our huge, timeless, loving Creator. He doesn't want you limiting His creation with your mean-spirited version of events. Tell your stories, but tell them truthfully and with kindness.

Let the Holy Spirit transform your heart to love so that the overabundance of what flows out of your heart—your stories—is also love. Let your heart be transformed by the grace of your Savior so that your stories are also filled with His grace.

THOUGHTS ABOUT THIS COMMANDMENT

1. Martin Luther's explanation of the Eighth Commandment is this: "We should fear and love God so that we do not tell lies about our neighbor, betray him, slander him, or hurt his reputation, but defend him, speak

well of him, and explain everything in the kindest way." Talk about the terms and words *tell lies*, *betray*, *slander*, and *hurt his reputation*. Are we still guilty of these today?

2. Luther tells us part of the Eighth Commandment is to "explain everything in the kindest way." Think about your relationships right now, including those with women with whom you don't get along very well. Talk about how you need God's help to approach these relationships with a kind and charitable mind-set. When you talk about these women, do you put things in the kindest, most positive terms you can, or do you use a slant that makes you look good?

Beat Up by Gossip

There are six things that the LORD hates, seven that are an abomination to Him: haughty eyes, a lying tongue, and hands that shed innocent blood, a heart that devises wicked plans, feet that make haste to run to evil, a false witness who breathes out lies, and one who sows discord among brothers.

—Solomon in Proverbs 6:16–19

THERE ARE TWO TYPES OF PEOPLE IN THE WORLD: those who don't remember middle school and those who can still smell the cafeteria floor wax because that place held their traumatizing moments. I'm in the second group. Middle school was a nightmare of sitting by myself in that cafeteria, being bullied, and being beaten up by gossip.

For elementary school, I went to a tiny Lutheran school with the same eight kids. When I graduated, I was excited for the big public middle school. I wanted a middle school experience like I had read about in *The Baby-Sitters Club*. I wanted to talk on the phone and have slumber parties where I giggled with my new friends about which boys we liked.

This is not what happened. I had no friends, no clue about fashion trends or MTV, and no thick skin. I walked into Weis Middle School with a giant target on my back. My hair was short and permed, and I hadn't learned how to shave my legs yet. A group of boys teased me constantly about this.

Eventually, some nice kids did invite me to sit at their lunch table. Two of those girls were Crystal Brown and Marie Mapleton.

Marie was born with spina bifida and was in a wheelchair. She was smart, funny, and so, so kind. She had gone to school with those bullies her whole life, and they accepted her. Marie was a friend to everyone—but especially to those of us infected with the middle school virus of being a little weird. I adored her.

Crystal Brown was also a little weird. She rarely smiled and came from a tough home. She cussed, told us crazy stories about her mom's weekend drinking binges, and was also fiercely loyal to Marie.

Most days during lunch, Crystal would rant about someone she didn't like. She always wanted to beat someone up. She and I weren't natural friends, but I was desperate to blend in, and Crystal craved attention. To my wimpy self, Crystal was a bit marvelous—and very intimidating.

When Crystal started calling me at night, I was beyond thrilled. Finally! A real friend and actual phone conversations. She would complain, and I would agree with her. Crystal was glad for a listener, and I was glad someone included me.

During one call, Crystal and I discussed the mean PE teacher who didn't like girls. He was so unfair, he was a male chauvinist, and the principal should fire him. Yes! I agreed. Of course! Definitely!

I chimed in that I hated PE and wished I didn't have to take the stupid class. I also said something about how lucky Marie was that she didn't have to deal with PE. Crystal let me go and hung up.

When I got off the bus at school the next morning, those bully boys greeted me with Crystal in their center. Her face was red, and before the bus driver even pulled away, Crystal started cussing me out. She said I was fake and that she had told Marie everything I had said about her.

What? What was she talking about?

As the bus driver parked, the rest of the seventh graders mobbed around us. I wiped at my tears, blurring their faces.

And then Crystal told me she was going to beat me up.

This drew everyone else in the parking lot over to us. Some of the kids chanted, "FIGHT! FIGHT!"

I couldn't run; the crowd was too thick around us. I asked, "Why are you doing this?"

Another girl yelled, "Because you're telling everyone Marie is too lazy to do PE!"

"Noooooo!" I whimpered. "That's not what I said!"

Crystal was breathing out of her nose and screaming that she was going to kick my butt. She had kicked the butts of other kids, right here in this parking lot. She would do it to me. Where were the teachers?

A nice kid, Keith, got in Crystal's face. He told her to calm down because she would get suspended if she hit me. Crystal shoved me down and then whirled around and told the circle of kids I wasn't worth it. The mob followed her over to the other side of the parking lot.

I cried, humiliated and terrified because I had almost been punched. And why? How could all those people believe something so obviously untrue?

For the rest of that miserable school year, Crystal told everyone what a fake I was. It was such a worn-out story, I can't imagine why everyone kept listening to her. Kids wrote in slam books that I was mean and that's why I had no friends. They told Marie not to sit with me at lunch—but she ignored them. By the end of that year, I wished Crystal *had* punched me. The gossip she spread about me was so much worse than a broken nose would have been.

Each of us has a story about a time we've been beaten up by gossip. Maybe it happened in middle school or maybe it happened today. Either way, gossip still hurts more than a punch in the nose.

Why in the world, then, do we keep gossiping? If I saw a mob beating up a woman in our school's parking lot, I would be sick. If women were bloodying her lips with their purses and spiking her in the gut with their high heels, the mob scene would be on the news.

But gossip? Stories about which mom is drunk by five every afternoon and who might be having an affair? Come and sit closer to me so I can hear all the details.

As women, are we really still living in this same mob mentality? Are we still naive enough to believe gossip doesn't hurt if it's not about us? Are we still using gossip as a slightly prettier way to beat up our enemies?

Help us stop, Lord. Give us a new pair of glasses to see gossip through Your eyes. Show us how it hurts the victim. But also, show us how gossiping hurts our soul, our faith. Help us see how gossip gives life to our pride—the one part of us that doesn't need inflating.

Lord, replace our hatred with the love of our Savior, our fighting with the peace of the Holy Spirit, and our pride with passion for You. Teach us, Father, to share Your passionate love with the world that desperately needs it.

YOUR STORY/GOD'S STORY

1. The Eighth Commandment might feel like the most harmless commandment. After all, God's not commanding us against killing or stealing; this one is just about talking. Think about our stories, especially our stories as women. How can our tongues be our most powerful weapons?

2. So let's say you really tried to follow the Eighth Commandment and stopped your part of spreading gossip. Would it be that effective? In other words, in such a mob-mentality kind of sin, does one person not spreading gossip really stop it? What good might this do?

3. If it's true we gossip to hurt people we don't like, what's the deeper sin here? Think back to the Fifth Commandment. Why doesn't God want us to hate others?

4. Martin Luther said, "When you get to know about a sin, let your ear become its grave and shovel the dirt in on top of it." Talk about this advice and also about Matthew 7:12. If you had done something wrong, how would you want those who heard about it to react?

5. Going forward, talk about what this commandment looks like in your relationships. Is there a specific friendship or a particular group of people in which you find yourself gossiping? How could you help defend those who are beat up by gossip?

PRAY . . .

Lord, You want to cover my relationships with Your love. But because of my pride, I use my words as weapons. Change my heart so the words that flow from it are kind and helpful. Thank You for the example of Jesus, who perfectly modeled putting everything in the kindest and most charitable way. In His redeeming name. Amen.

The Ugly Stepchild
of Church Missions

And we know that for those who love God all things work together for good, for those who are called according to His purpose.

—Paul in Romans 8:28

WHEN WE WERE NEW TO KATY and looking for a church home, we visited one of the biggest, shiniest churches in town. The pastor preached for forty-five minutes, and let me tell you, he was *bringing it*. No one in the huge worship center moved while he delivered the best sermon about the prodigal son I've ever heard.

But the church was so massive that worship felt like a One Direction concert, which was definitely not our style.

Then we learned that this church was opening a tiny mission congregation in a high school gym close to our house. We visited that campus and immediately knew we had found our church home. The pastor's sermon was still captivating, but the congregation had only a hundred people. We signed up that day to be charter members of this little church plant.

If you've ever been part of a church plant, you know the hard work that goes into making it happen every week. Over the next two years, our rag-tag volunteers did it all: handed out fliers at the mall, transformed a high school cafeteria into a sanctuary, played in the band, and taught Sunday School. These people became our friends, and this church became our life. We worked hard to welcome every visitor and to make worship at our church warm and engaging. We were so proud of our little congregation.

But the main campus never seemed to give us any credit. No one from that congregation ever visited us or came to our events. They didn't know about the donuts we carefully arranged or the Sunday School lessons we carefully prepared or the hardened atheists who wanted to be baptized. The board just wanted reports about what our attendance was every week.

This hurt our feelings, and we joked that our little congregation was the ugly stepchild of the main church. The two campuses were like distant siblings who shared a last name and the same parent board of directors. The similarities ended there, though. The main campus had a huge, gorgeous facility and lots of money; we carried our church around in a trailer and set up where we could. We wanted to build a building, but the board of directors said we weren't stable yet, not until we had two hundred members.

We never got two hundred members. After months of politics and our pastor arguing with the board over money, they announced they were shutting us down. They didn't think our congregation would ever get two hundred members, and the church was losing money on us.

A majority of church start-ups don't make it to the building stage, and I'm sure the volunteers at those campuses feel the same way we did: controlled, angry, and sad. Our little church family was devastated.

For months, our group of volunteers acted like the survivors of a train wreck. We wanted to forget the whole experience, but we could not stop talking about it. In group texts and in living rooms, we trashed the people who had closed our campus. They were the tyrants; we were the martyrs. We told these stories to one another and to anyone who would listen. Then we waited for relief that never came.

Our family joined a new church, and we arrived every Sunday like the angry kids from an ugly divorce. Pastor Davis, our new pastor, must have felt sorry for Mike and me. Sewage was swirling in our spirits, and it was spilling out in our stories. We talked about our old church all the time, like kids telling the same knock-knock jokes everyone has heard.

But Pastor Davis was kind and cared for us in the exact way we needed. He gave us time to get over the train wreck, but he also introduced us to the church members we needed to meet, older men and women who had been members since Kennedy was president. These sweet couples welcomed our kids into the Sunday School classrooms where they themselves had learned about Jesus, where they had taught, where their own kids had learned. The smell of ancient incense and their sweet care were the balm our blistered souls needed.

Our church closing taught me about the importance of stories. I learned and I'm learning that we believe the stories we tell ourselves. We decide if we're victims or if we're loved. We can either create drama with our stories or we can help others. We can either tell the same worn-out tales about those who have hurt us or we can trust God that our lives are not this one-dimensional.

When God tells us not to lie about others, He reminds us that the stories we tell matter. What mirror do your stories hold up to your life? Do you use them to boost your own ego? Have you mastered the art of telling half-truths to paint your enemies the colors you think they should be?

You belong to God. He loves you. Let your stories show that sacred identity. Let your stories tell the world the greatest story ever, the story of a God who loved His people so much that He sent His Son, Jesus, to save them from their sins. That is the beginning and happy ending of your life story!

YOUR STORY/GOD'S STORY

1. The Eighth Commandment protects you and others because it doesn't allow anyone to freeze one moment in time or to freeze a single perception of another person. God is more loving and creative than that. What story are you telling yourself that shrinks another person down to a villain instead of a soul?

2. When you tell a one-dimensional story about someone else, it doesn't quite ring true. How does telling this story also damage you? How does it show a lack of faith in God's plans for your life and theirs?

3. Talk about Matthew 18:15–18. Jesus tells us to talk face-to-face with the people who have hurt us instead of gossiping. How is this so much harder? Think about Jesus' ministry. How did He model Matthew 18?

4. Read about Potiphar's wife in Genesis 39. This woman was obsessed with Joseph and wanted to control him. When Joseph wouldn't do what she wanted, she told lies about him. Potiphar's wife seems like one of the most desperate and mean women in the Bible. But are we also guilty of her sins of control and cruelty when we gossip today? How is gossip a control issue?

5. The explanation of this commandment says we should not lie about, betray, or slander our neighbor or hurt his reputation. These seem like really strong words for gossip, but when we tell stories with villains and victims, we slander the people we don't like. Think about the ways you're using stories in your life right now. How could you improve them so you're not using them to slander?

PRAY . . .

Lord, You are always gracious, always loving, always generous. Because I'm desperate for control, I tell ugly lies and half-truths. Help me to see I'm not a victim, Lord, but that You love and totally accept me. Through the sacrifice of Your Son, You see me as perfect and forgiven. In His redeeming name. Amen.

Camp Love Triangle

Therefore, having put away falsehood, let each one of you speak the truth with his neighbor, for we are members one of another.

—Paul in Ephesians 4:25

THE VERY BEST AND WORST PART OF MY JOB is speaking to women's groups. I love the speaking part, but the worst part is that I feel like I leave unfinished business. It's difficult for me to leave after connecting, whether I've been there for just one evening or for a full weekend. While the cleanup crew is sweeping the floor, a woman will stop me to chat about a problem, and I'm terrible at spontaneous advice. I'm a deep thinker, and I end up giving lame, quick replies that I know aren't very helpful.

Then, on the drive home, I always think of the perfect answer for the young mom who is struggling to make it to church or the older mom who is restless now that her kids have left home. I'll probably never see either one again, and I regret that perhaps I've let them down.

This happened a few summers ago when a camp invited me to share devotions with the campers and Bible studies with the staff. I arrived at the very end of summer, just a couple of weeks before the counselors would go back to their colleges. This incredible group of counselors had worked twenty-three hours a day, six days a week, for two months, and they were all ragged.

Heather and Casey, two beautiful, vivacious girls, were especially so. As an added complication, both of them were in love with Josh, a six four, square-shouldered quarterback. He was as funny as Jimmy Fallon and as down-to-earth as Conan O'Brien, and he had the boy-next-door looks of Seth Meyers. I accidentally stepped right in the middle of the girls' catfight over him.

After breakfast the second day, Heather plopped down across from me and told me her story. Josh had come to camp with Casey, his girlfriend. They had been a couple for three years and would probably get engaged. According to Heather, this was a huge mistake. Casey was a jealous psychopath, which was the reason Josh had broken up with her three weeks into the summer.

And then he had hooked up with Heather.

And then he had gone back to Casey.

Heather was the light of the camp, the sparkly ball of charisma the other staff orbited. With her willowy figure and captivating tenor, she could be the next Taylor Swift. When she sang "Jesus Loves Me" at campfire, we all sat in stunned silence. No one even breathed. She was full of pulsating energy and talent—and she was lovesick over Josh.

Heather cried through her whole story. "I think he loves me. He keeps going back to Casey because she's so controlling. He is making the biggest mistake of his life."

I hugged her, got her a glass of water, told her this was a rough way to end the summer, and offered to pray with her.

As I prayed, Heather ugly-cried, her nose running and her shoulders shaking. "We're in love. He is the one. Why is he being so stupid?"

I wanted to tell Heather to stay far away from Josh and this drama. I wanted to point out that she didn't know Casey's side of the story. I wanted Heather to see that she had so much to offer the world—her leadership, her charisma, her voice—and she could do anything she wanted.

But she wouldn't have listened because she wasn't really asking for advice. She just needed a listener. She needed to take out the garbage that was stinking up her mind.

The next night, Casey sat next to me at campfire worship. Afterward, she asked if we could talk, and I suggested a night hike. She, too, was vibrating with the need to vent. I think she would have agreed to a night of swimming in the swampy lake if it meant I would listen to her make sense of her swirling emotions.

We navigated the trails with flashlights, tripping over fallen branches and stepping over roots that looked like sleeping snakes. Halfway down the trail,

Casey opened up a vein of pain. Over the three years she and Josh had dated, her parents had divorced, and his sister had committed suicide. They had helped her mom move out of her childhood home. Casey had cried with Josh for hours after he got the call that his sister was dead. They had come to faith in Jesus together. "We have been through the worst year. This summer was supposed to be our fresh start. And he slept with Heather. I hate her."

This kind of crazy, scared, angry storytelling marked my teen years too. To find a sympathetic listener was to find a break from my own confused mind. These girls needed to talk like they needed to breathe. All I could offer was sympathy, silence, hugs, and prayers. When Casey slipped into her cabin after midnight, I think she was healed from telling her story; she looked like she had just returned from the spa.

This is the power of story, of talking it out, of opening the vein of pain. But were these girls also gossiping? Had I done the wrong thing by just listening? Their stories were black-and-white, rigid, with no grace for each other. They didn't just want my prayers—they wanted my indignation and disgust. Did I wimp out by not urging them to tell better stories?

The next day was the end of the week, time for the campers to go home and the counselors to get a day off. Heather squealed out of the parking lot in her VW, the top down and the backseat crowded with friends. I packed my car, sad for all of them, frustrated with myself for not helping.

Jilly, the camp director, was a no-nonsense nursing student from Oregon. She was earthy and wise. She taught kids about Jesus in the summer, and she was starting a new job as an ER nurse in September.

Before I left, I helped her clean out the staff break room. I told her I always found myself in this same position, of listening but not really helping. I asked her what advice she gave this beehive of teen angst.

Here's the advice Jilly gave me that made so much sense: Telling stories is like driving—it's good and necessary and it gets us to a new place. But we have to watch out so we're not speeding. When you're speeding, you're out of control. Just like gossiping, when you start speeding, you need to slow down before you hurt someone.

I wondered if this is how Jesus also saw gossip. He talked to thousands of people, listened to their stories, cried with them, held them, and comforted them. But He didn't let them get stuck at the damaging part of their stories. He gently nudged them back to His Gospel perspective: repentance and forgiveness, promises and truth.

God's view of our lives is full of love, grace, and miracles. God's story is the one we all need to hear. When a friend starts speeding with gossip, this is the reminder we can give her.

I hope God can help me get better at this. I want to share His love with people who need to take the garbage out of their minds. I want to show them their reflection in the Law and point them to repentance. Most of all, I want to tell them that Jesus, in His mercy, will heal their veins of pain and provide peace greater than what any of us can even understand.

YOUR STORY/GOD'S STORY

1. When you're angry, you gossip because you see only your perspective. Talk about a conflict you had last year, or five years ago, or even ten years ago. In hindsight, how was your perspective limited? Now think about God's all-knowing perspective of our lives. Why do you think this commandment is so important to our loving Father?

2. There's a fine line between verbal processing and gossiping. Talk about your experience with this. Is it kinder to listen to a woman who needs to vent or better to walk away from the gossip?

3. Read 1 Timothy 5:12–13. In Paul's letter to Timothy, he tells the young pastor that women with too much time on their hands will become "gossips and busybodies" (v. 13). Why do you think this is? Where is the truth in this for you?

4. Read Luke 10:38–42. Read the story of Martha telling Jesus about Mary. Tired from working all day, Martha was frustrated because her sister wasn't helping. We've all felt this frustration before. Read verse 41 again. How did Jesus respond? Did He let Martha stay in her anger, or did He move her on to another perspective?

5. In the explanation of this commandment, Luther tells us not to gossip, but also that we should "explain everything in the kindest way." Wow.

This can seem impossible when you're angry and only able to see your own hurt and your enemy's faults. But this next step is so important in our relationship with God. Think about your life right now. Where do you need God to help you to see another person through His eyes so you can explain everything in the kindest way with regard to your relationship?

PRAY . . .

Heavenly Father, You love every single person in the world so much. Help me to see my enemies through Your eyes. Help me to delight in Your love and not hurt others. Help me to tell stories that are true. Help me to love others with the love Jesus has for us. In His redeeming name. Amen.

A Manifesto
to Stop
All the Lying

"If You abide in My word, you are truly My disciples, and you will know the truth, and the truth will set you free."

—Jesus in John 8:31–32

REMEMBER PLAYING TRUTH OR DARE? Wasn't it thrilling to hear your friends tell the absolute truth? *Really, she was held back in the first grade? She still wets the bed? She feels like she doesn't have any friends?*

The thrilling part wasn't only hearing everyone else's confessions, it was also the freedom to say your own truth out loud. You could open your mouth and admit, "I'm really afraid my parents will get a divorce," or "I make myself throw up after I eat," or "I'm not sure what I believe about God." There was no danger of the confession leaving the group because everyone had told the truth. You all were on equal ground.

Let's bring the absolute truth back into our conversations. All of us. Let's stop lying and agree to tell each other exactly what we're afraid of and exactly what's going on in our lives.

God tells us not to bear false witness against our neighbors, but how many of us bear false witness against ourselves? How many of us join in with women who are telling perfectly untrue stories about their lives to make themselves look perfect? What's our response? We tell perfectly untrue stories about our own lives.

But this is not working for any of us. We need to honestly tell the stories of our lives—about the five cups of coffee I drink or about the five glasses of wine you drink. Maybe then we could get help. Maybe then we could pray for one another.

I used to be the worst offender of not telling the truth. I exaggerated everything so the person I was talking to would like me. Remember how you felt when you were thirteen years old and talking to your crush? That's how I felt when I talked to other women. *Like me! Like me! Like me!* It was exhausting for them and exhausting for me.

When I turned forty, I vowed to start telling the truth—first to myself about how I was really feeling and then to others about my fears and shortcomings.

For a long time, I tiptoed around the shore of being a truth teller. I was too scared. I dipped my toe in the water but then walked away. Then one day, I finally I dove in. I started looking other women in the eye and saying, "I have a lot of anxiety, and I can't seem to relax. Even when nothing stressful is happening, my mind is running around and screaming. Lots of times, I'm not very nice to my family because I need so much quiet in my mind. They talk a lot, and I just want them to stop. When they don't, I'm kind of mean."

Other women said the very best words they could to me: "Yes. Me too. I understand."

Jesus taught this over and over: tell the truth, tell the truth, tell the truth. He didn't tolerate exaggerating, white lies, or half-truths. When teaching everyone from tax collectors to prostitutes, from the Pharisees to His own disciples, His message was the same: do not live a lie.

Jesus told the woman at the well that to change her life, she had to be honest about her five husbands. He called out to Zacchaeus and told him to make his dishonest life right. Before Jesus called Peter to ministry, He confronted His disciple about how he had denied Him the night before His crucifixion.

Consider the Eighth Commandment God's command and invitation to live a truthful life. God hates lying because He knows the damage it causes and the damage it covers up. Avoiding your hard issues by lying is like taking an aspirin for your brain cancer. Your Father is the best oncologist on the planet, and He wants to heal your deep issues. But if you're not admitting your problems, you're covering them up. You're taking aspirin for cancer.

Jesus said the truth can set you free. He wants you to live authentically. Just like He told the Samaritan woman, Zacchaeus, and Peter, He wants you to know that He will forgive you for everything. You don't have to live an image.

God wants you to know that perfection is a lie and true freedom comes from living under His grace. God wants you to dare to tell the truth that you really need the forgiveness, love, and hope that comes from His Son.

YOUR STORY/GOD'S STORY

1. Talk about your relationships. In which ones are you not comfortable telling the truth right now? What does that tell you about these relationships or about yourself?

2. Perhaps the reason we don't tell the truth is because we don't want God or anyone else to tell us that we have to change our lives. Read Luke 19:1–10, the story of Zacchaeus. How did this dishonest tax collector change when Jesus confronted him? If God were to confront you about a dishonest part of your life right now, what would He want you to change? In what ways would this change be uncomfortable—and ultimately helpful?

3. Tell the story about a time you cried out to God with your absolute truth. Maybe it was during a season when you were lying in other places. What caused the lies? What relief did you find in telling the truth?

4. Read John 4:1–45. The woman at the well did what we all do when we want to impress our audience—she lied. But Jesus reveals the truth of her chaotic personal life. Then He tells her the whole truth about her husbands (v. 19). Finally, she professes her faith in Jesus (v. 39). What do you notice about this progression? How important is it for believers to tell the truth about our lives? Is confession still an important part of a Christian's life?

5. When you exaggerate and tell white lies about your life, you betray who you really are. This is never how Jesus wanted you to live. Talk about a lie you tell about your life so you look different than how you really are. How can you lead a life that doesn't lie about your true self?

PRAY . . .

Heavenly Father, You are truth and love. Anchor me to Your love,
Lord, so I'm secure. Help my words be true, Lord. Help my stories
show my identity in You. Thank You for the gift of Your Son, who
forgives my sin and lets me live in Your forgiveness. In His redeeming
name. Amen.

Don't Covet Your Neighbor's Things

"You shall not covet your neighbor's house."

—God in Exodus 20:17

And He said, "What comes out of a person is what defiles him. For from within, out of the heart of man, come evil thoughts, sexual immorality, theft, murder, adultery, coveting, wickedness, deceit, sensuality, envy, slander, pride, foolishness. All these evil things come from within, and they defile a person."

—Jesus in Mark 7:20–23

THIS COMMANDMENT. This is the one that God could have named the Great Commandment of the Twenty-First Century. When God commanded against coveting, He was telling His people not to envy their neighbors for their houses, servants, or animals. But He was undoubtedly looking ahead to the culture of coveting that the information age has created.

What a strange time in history. Social media and constant advertising preach that you're on a quest for a prettier life, an easier life, a more meaningful and productive life than the one God has given you.

This culture is what makes "do not covet" the Great Commandment of the Twenty-First Century. When the first women tried to follow all the Ten Commandments, they struggled in the same ways we do. Kids have always had trouble honoring their parents, our human hearts have always found idols to worship, and gossip has been a perpetual problem.

But the Ninth and Tenth Commandments are different. Thanks to the collective one billion hours the world spends on social media every day, we are relating to each other differently than before. Asking yourself if all that scrolling makes you covet your neighbor's life is like asking yourself if smoking hurts your lungs.

Now more than ever before, we need God to say to us, "I've given you what I want you to have, and that's it. The blessings I've given everyone else are forbidden fruit. Stop wanting them."

This is exactly what God tells us in the Ninth Commandment.

Trusting that God has given each of us perfect gifts is countercultural. But let's do that. Let's trust that He is taking care of us every single second. Let's stop spending more on what advertisers tell us we should want, and let's stop wasting our time peeking in on what our neighbors have.

Really, the only way to live—in the first century or the twenty-first—is to trust that every moment of your life is an exciting adventure and a gift from your heavenly Father. Celebrate this life, celebrate your status as His redeemed child, and celebrate these exact blessings He's given you.

Yes, let's live like that.

THOUGHTS ABOUT THIS COMMANDMENT

1. Luther explains this commandment this way: "We should fear and love God so that we do not scheme to get our neighbor's inheritance or house, or get it in a way which only appears right, but help and be of service to him in keeping it." Talk about how this explanation shows something deeper than just our actions. What does it look like to trust that God has given you the good and perfect gifts intended just for you? If you're content with your gifts, how will this affect your actions, including any scheming to get your neighbor's house or inheritance?

2. The second part of Luther's explanation might sound a little strange. How are you supposed to help another woman keep her house? As you talk more about this commandment, talk about ways you could help others keep what God has given them.

The Lie of the Pie

Now to Him who is able to do far more abundantly than all that we ask or think, according to the power at work within us, to Him be glory in the church and in Christ Jesus throughout all generations, forever and ever. Amen.

—Paul in Ephesians 3:20–21

IMAGINE YOU'VE JUST ARRIVED at a huge dinner party with lots of your friends and also some strangers. Everyone is starving. The hostess announces she's serving only her special apple pie and begins cutting a gorgeous tart that smells like cinnamon and baked apples. Everyone watches as she hands out pieces. You cringe as some of the pushy guests get plate-size slices. You watch as they gobble up the brown crust dripping with thick apples and speckled with cinnamon.

No! If they get all that pie, what does that leave for you?

Without enough pie, *that's* where it leaves you.

Most of us see life in exactly this way. Everything good in this world is a pie, and we need to fight for the biggest piece. We should covet the bigger slices our neighbors have because this means less pie for us. If only I had *her* thick slice, dripping with appley goodness, then I would be more happy/productive/important. Each of us believes the Lie of the Pie in some area of our lives—the idea that more for your neighbor means less for you. For me, I believe the Lie of the Pie most in my career.

I've discovered the hard way that envy is not only a stomachache in your soul, but it also makes you act pretty stupid. Ten years ago, at a writers conference, a friend and I got tipsy before the big awards dinner. We were obnoxious.

We laughed at the other writers' acceptance speeches and over-the-top outfits. Our companions shushed us, but I was so envious of those writers on the stage, and I felt strangely brash. My ugly envy fueled the whole night, and it still embarrasses me.

I felt out of my mind that night, even without the glasses of cheap wine. Jealousy was a steroid shot right to my insecurities. I wanted someone to call me onto a stage and tell me I was a good writer. I wanted their pie. Because of this envy and shame, I dropped out of the conference circuit for years.

But the truth was, avoiding conferences wasn't helping my jealousy. It just allowed me to bury it deeper inside me, where it blossomed into a growing panic. Every time another writer's blog went viral or another author got a great book contract, I felt like I was at a Black Friday sale and was the only one missing out on the $10 iPads.

Then I learned that there was a Christian writers conference coming up where lots of my favorite authors were speaking. I admitted to Mike that I wanted to go, but I couldn't handle the jealousy.

He told me every conference is like this. Anytime you're crowded together with your professional peers, you start to feel insecure. He doesn't like going to software conferences because he feels as though he's not as good as the other consultants. Another friend told me teacher conferences are the worst. She goes to them to feel inspired, but she ends up coming home sick with envy about another teacher who taught her four-year-olds to read. She said professional jealousy at conferences is as common as nametags and free bottles of water.

So I went to the conference, ready for the envy ulcer. I showed up for the sessions and listened to my favorite authors talk about publishing, bracing myself for the shame of all the unpublished books on my computer at home. I waited to crave their pieces of pie, frantic that they were gobbling up my share.

But this conference was different. There was no awards ceremony, and every one of the speakers was so kind. They stood on the stage and told us all of their writing secrets. They told us how proud they were of us for showing up.

They didn't stop there. These successful writers, who had experienced epic sales and epic fails, hugged every one of us. They kept telling all of us, "You are doing such a good job. You are so incredibly brave to keep writing. How can we help you?"

These writers saw their careers as vocations, as gifts from God. Their identity wasn't based on what the person next to them had; their identity was based on what God had actually given them. These writers believed God would keep blessing them abundantly. There was no pie we were fighting over—there was a whole pie buffet, where we could go back for more and more and more. God could never run out of pie.

When I came home refreshed from the conference, I realized how my envy had metastasized to my relationships. Another writer told me she was just about to quit her blog. She wasn't getting many hits, and she felt pretty dejected. My envy made me feel relieved she was quitting. My self-centered math added this up to equal more readers for me—which is incredibly weird and stupid math.

But instead of buying into the lie that there's a finite pie of success, I invited her to meet for coffee. We both told stories of blogs we'd written and hoped would set the Internet on fire but barely got a click. Each of us left the conversation lighter, less afraid. Talking to her shrank my pride-swollen perspective.

We're all guilty of believing the Lie of the Pie. We're stingy with our encouragement because we're afraid more success for her means less for me. Our human minds don't understand God's infinite math.

Ask the Holy Spirit to teach you this simple formula: God gives you infinite blessings, and He gives infinite blessings to your neighbor too. This adds up to the best math ever.

Thank our loving God that there is no division in His formulas. It's all multiplication—Him blessing us exponentially with His grace and the love of our Savior. Because we have the blessings of Baptism, we are His new creations (2 Corinthians 5:17). Because He loves us, He gives us living water that never runs out or leaves us thirsty (John 4:13). He assures us that His "steadfast love . . . never ceases; His mercies never come to an end; they are new every morning" (Lamentations 3:22–23).

YOUR STORY/GOD'S STORY

1. When have you believed the Lie of the Pie? In your work, or in your relationships, do you fall into the trap of thinking there is not enough success to go around?

2. When have you felt jealous and self-righteous, believing God runs out of blessings? Read the parable of the prodigal son in Luke 15:11–32. Talk about how we sometimes act like the older son, believing we have been cheated out of our share and refusing to join the party.

3. God's infinite math is shown in Mark 6:30–44, when Jesus feeds the five thousand. Read verse 35 to see His disciples' panicky reaction to the crowd and how they are worried about running out. But Jesus teaches them His new math and tells them they *can* feed the people—and they can feed them well. Next, the disciples organize the people into groups, and everyone shares. God creates freely, the disciples distribute freely, and the people share freely. What does this teach us about how to treat the blessings God has given each of us?

4. Read Deuteronomy 15:7–10 and 2 Corinthians 9:5. Talk about how our desire and our coveting lead to destruction and selfishness. How do you see coveting as an enemy to generosity in your life?

5. One of the key words in the explanation of this commandment is *service*: "We should fear and love God so that we do not scheme to get our neighbor's inheritance or house, or get it in a way which only appears right, but help and be of *service* to him in keeping it." Think about the ways God has blessed you. Could you share some of your blessings to serve a person who is struggling? Share your thoughts.

PRAY . . .

Lord, Your love and gifts are abundant; they will never run out. So often, I see my blessings as finite. Give me eyes to see Your math, Father. Give me a heart to trust Your providence. Give me a soul that celebrates Your Son. In His redeeming name. Amen.

Instagram &
Chocolate Cake Pops

And they sent their disciples to Him, along with the Herodians, saying, "Teacher, we know that You are true and teach the way of God truthfully, and You do not care about anyone's opinion, for You are not swayed by appearances."

—Jesus' disciples in Matthew 22:16

I TURNED FORTY-ONE LAST WEEK, and I celebrated like anyone who wants to feel instantly festive—by eating lots and lots of cake. Carrot-cake cupcakes with cream cheese frosting with my family, thick slices of German chocolate cake with my parents, and red velvet cake balls at a lunch with my friends. The more cake I ate, the more I craved. When I wasn't out celebrating, I was at home, snacking on leftover cake.

Until all that cake caught up with me. A sugar coma fogged up my brain, my heart was always racing, and I couldn't fall asleep. By Friday, I was like a patient in the psych ward or the mother of a newborn. My week was busy, and if I didn't lay off the cake, I would feel like someone who was showing up on the morning of a marathon stumbling drunk.

But cake was suddenly everywhere. The barista handed me a sample of pink cake pop with my chamomile tea, and I popped it into my mouth so fast she gasped. My kids didn't like the chocolate frosting at a birthday party, and I gladly finished all three pieces of their cake. The more cake I ate, the more I craved. Afterward, my stomach churned from the sugar, but I didn't care. I could not quit the cake. The spinach salad I usually eat for lunch seemed tasteless compared with the flavor explosion of the strawberry shortcake I had for dessert.

I'm as equally addicted to social media as I am to cake, and scrolling through Facebook or Instagram messes with me the same way eating cake does. My heart rushes with envy, I'm twitchy to post comments that will get likes, and my mind clouds with the monotonous pictures of strangers' lives. I sit in social-media stupor while real life swirls around me, but I cannot quit these websites.

My cake craving starts with my tongue tingling for sweetness. My social media craving starts with my brain tingling to disconnect from reality and connect to fantasy. Maybe it's different for you, but I never want to check Instagram while I'm playing tag with my kids or when I'm breathless from laughing so hard with my husband.

It's during the mind-numbingly boring moments that I crave social media. Faced with a sink full of dishes or an evening of monitoring my kids' homework, I'm powerless against the urge to scroll. Basically, my hours on social media are a long, exhausting exercise in skipping hours of real, actual life.

But here's the truth: The real, actual moments of my life are precious. My minutes, hours, and days are literally little gifts from God (Ephesians 5:15–17). When God gave me these four kids, this husband, a soul that needs to write, a mom who loves to chat, and neighbors who don't know Jesus, He did it for a reason. God gave me all this because He meant for me to stay present in this one and only precious life He's given me. Slipping out to peek in the windows of other lives was never His plan. Disconnecting from God's clear calling to serve this husband and these kids so I can envy my friends' Pinterest projects is a sin.

My craving to engage in a fake world, one where dozens of near-strangers tell me I'm good, is as strong as my craving to stuff my mouth full of chocolate frosting and spongy yellow cake. My craving to believe your life is better than mine is as strong as my craving to lick the frosting off a Key lime cupcake.

But I'm learning more and more that this pastime is like the snake in the Garden of Eden. Social media whispers that my real life isn't enough, that my family, my talents, and my blessings are not enough. Social media whispers that I need more. This is coveting. This is the creation telling the Creator that

He doesn't understand what His creation really needs.

As I'm trying to detox from social media, I'm discovering God's wisdom that gratitude and trust are our antidotes against envy. If only Eve would have told the snake, "I don't need to eat that fruit. I have this whole garden from God, and I trust that's enough."

Can we also see we don't need the forbidden fruit of our friends' lives that social media offers?

My prayer is that we would understand the Gospel, that we would understand that God has made us alive in Christ (Ephesians 2:4–5). He has shown and will keep showing us the immeasurable riches of His grace. Each and every day of my life and your life is important, precious, and unique.

Each day is another day alive in Christ.

YOUR STORY/GOD'S STORY

1. If you could describe social media in one word, what would it be? Do you find it addictive? destructive? mind-numbing? Do you think it fuels your envy? How might this pollute your relationship with God?

2. Read Psalm 34:8, and talk about what the Lord has done and is doing in your life. As you talk about this, tell how believing in God's abundance is about appreciating what God has already given you and trusting that He will continue to give you the exact, perfect gifts. How can gratitude become more a part of your life?

3. Raise your hand if you find yourself using social media to get attention instead of real connection. Talk about this. When we aim for likes, we try to create a lifestyle that makes others covet what we have. This is exactly what God commands against in the Ninth Commandment. Read Psalm 96:1–9 and Psalm 115:1. Who deserves the glory?

4. Is social media all bad? Or could it be used as a tool to spread the message of Jesus Christ to the world? Social media is a waiting, diverse, worldwide audience. Look at Matthew 28:16–20. What message does Jesus want us to share with those in darkness? How do you—or how can you—use social media to tell the most important news in the history of the world to the people who need to hear it?

5. Coveting begins as a seed in your heart and blooms into your actions. In the explanation of this commandment, Luther writes, "We should fear and love God so that we do not scheme to get our neighbor's inheritance or house." Talk about the word *scheme*. How does your coveting lead you to crafty scheming for the forbidden fruit of another life?

PRAY . . .

Heavenly Father, thank You for blessing me with the exact home, life, and gifts You want me to have. Forgive me for lusting after what others have. Encourage me to find my worth in You, Lord. Tune my heart so I crave the love of my Savior, Jesus. In His redeeming name. Amen.

Shiny Gold
Glitter Dust

Now to Him who is able to do far more abundantly than all that we ask or think, according to the power at work within us, to Him be glory in the church and in Christ Jesus throughout all generations, forever and ever. Amen.

—Paul in Ephesians 3:20–21

I MET EMILY WHEN I WAS NEW TO THE PRESCHOOL and a young mom. I was unsure of myself, so when Emily asked me to coffee and then started inviting my kids over for playdates, I felt like I had won some kind of friend mega jackpot. I didn't know yet that she would be my self-esteem kryptonite.

Emily had the Gwyneth Paltrow ability to always make exactly the right choice. Her kids were Doris and Hazel, which sounded like weird little-girl names—until you saw these girls. They were china dolls come to life, with shiny blond hair, wide-set blue eyes, and ivory skin. Doris and Hazel, of course. Exactly perfect.

Emily came from money and married into money. Everything about her was shiny. She was a little older than I was and seemed to have lived three lifetimes. Emily knew things: how to get front-row seats for George Strait, the best week to take the family to Vail, and how to throw a party that ten four-year-olds would remember forever.

I never knew who I was around Emily. She was bright red lipstick, big blond hair, and flowing, expensive clothes. The shininess of her swallowed me up; I seemed to disappear in her presence.

To be clear, the problem was not Emily at all. She was a loyal friend, asked great questions, told self-deprecating jokes, and always put others before herself. The problem was my insecurity and my coveting. Emily's life looked effortless. Emily's house was more comfortable. Emily's family enjoyed one another more. Emily's husband helped out more.

I imagined how I would fit into Emily's life. I was absolutely convinced that if I were like her, I would have more friends, my kids wouldn't be sick as often, and my husband would tell me I was pretty. Emily was painted in shiny gold glitter dust, and I was desperate for some of it to rub off on me.

But it never did. And it always seemed like she knew I wasn't really myself when we were together. Over Christmas break, when I switched grocery stores to her favorite and cut my hair in her same layered shag, she looked freaked out. By Valentine's Day, she had stopped texting me and didn't make eye contact at preschool pickup.

This was kind of a relief because I was so tired from loving her life and hating my own. Apparently, I had learned nothing from watching after-school specials as a kid. I still had not learned that the number-one rule of friendship is to be yourself.

In other bad self-esteem news, I was also friends with another woman named Laura, who was *not* covered in shiny gold glitter dust. Laura was overweight, shy, and had inherited her German father's nose. If Emily was an artisan chocolate, Laura was meat loaf and mashed potatoes.

She also volunteered hundreds of hours every year, bought thoughtful gifts, prayed for everyone, and was a great listener. She was a workhorse and absolutely the woman you wanted as your kid's Class Mom. She was sturdy, dependable, and the first to volunteer to run the kindergarten bake sale.

I liked Laura. When I talked to Laura, I felt like Glenda the Good Witch, giving Dorothy her most important life advice. She agreed with everything I said. My self-confidence soared around her.

But the weirdest part about being friends with Laura was that she told me all the time that she wanted my life. I think I was her shiny gold glitter dust. She wished she were as skinny as me, that her kids were as smart as mine, and that they lived in a house in our neighborhood.

When she told me this, I felt sorry for her and really sorry for her family. Couldn't she see how fantastic they were? Laura had a big bear of a husband who laughed hard and worked hard and loved Laura so much. Her kids were the sweetest in the class. And her house was so charming and so comfortable; I visited once and never wanted to leave her overstuffed couch.

Laura was insecure in the same way I am. I want to attach myself to anything that looks more successful and become a parasite. My insecurity keeps me believing I need only to find the right source to be content. This kind of insecurity acts like water: it finds the low spots, settles in, and does long-term damage. My friendship with Emily certainly had damaged me. I'm still ashamed at how quickly I started craving what she had.

An insecure woman's identity is not rooted in her Savior but in how she relates to everyone around her. Insecure women are the worst coveters because we are always looking for a new, better identity.

God wants us to know we are valuable because we are His children, through Baptism into faith in Jesus. We belong to Him. This is where your value comes from, not from the woman next to you.

Insecurity is a lifelong disease and as impossible to heal as a cold sore. Just when we believe we've finally quit the comparing habit, it pops up again someplace else.

But God wants to heal your deepest identity crises. He wants to fill you up with so much of His love that you don't need to scrounge around, looking for a better identity. He wants you to be so sure He has claimed you as His precious child that you refuse to cling to what this world offers.

Pray that you could better understand what it means to be God's child. Ask Him to overflow your heart with contentment so you need none of this world's shiny gold glitter dust.

YOUR STORY / GOD'S STORY

1. Tell your story about how your insecurity has led to coveting. Do you feel needy and insecure around some women and confident around others? What's the problem with this? Can you trace your coveting back to your weak identity?

2. If you're a people pleaser, you feel valuable when others like you. If you're competitive, you feel valuable when you beat the woman next to you. If you work hard on your image, you feel valuable when the world sees you as doing well. Talk about the problems with this.

3. As sinful humans, we find our value in all the wrong places. Talk about some of the lessons you've learned from finding your value in another person, in the stuff you have, or in your own abilities. Read Ephesians 3:17–18 and talk about what it means for Christ to live in your heart.

4. Read Psalm 139 and Hebrews 13:21. You are fearfully and wonderfully made! Make a list of what you're thankful God has given you. How do you use your unique talents to serve Him? Are there other ways you could serve God?

5. When we fear and love God, we trust Him and trust that He has given us good and perfect gifts. Where do you have trouble seeing that in your life right now? How can you see your home through eyes of gratitude rather than envy?

PRAY . . .

Lord, Your grace and Your forgiveness make me valuable. Even though You love me completely, I find my value in what the world says is good. Lord, help me to see myself the way You see me, through the blood and sacrifice of Your Son. In His redeeming name. Amen.

The Grass Is Greener under the Chicken Coop

And my God will supply every need of yours according to His riches in glory in Christ Jesus.

—Paul in Philippians 4:19

HAVE YOU NOTICED THAT DIFFERENT PARTS of the country have different One Day Goals? That is, each community embraces a collective dream about the ideal lifestyle they'd like to live "one day."

Depending on where you're living right now, your friends and neighbors have decided the One Day Goal might be to live in an industrial loft or in a renovated farmhouse or in a mountainside cabin.

When we lived in urban Houston, the One Day Goal of our friends and neighbors was to move to a small town around Austin. The Texas Hill Country is filled with funky little cities that ooze charm. Round Rock. Boerne. Gruene. The shared belief of those who live in downtown Houston is that anyone with sense at all should one day renovate a farmhouse in the Hill Country.

When I lived in Northern California, the One Day Goal was to move to a mountainside town. Everyone wanted to make enough money to retire to a small cabin with a fantastic view of the Sierra Nevada ridge and with Shakespeare festivals and hiking trails right nearby.

In Katy, Texas, the goal is to move to a farm in the middle of nowhere. Katy is, perhaps, the most suburban suburb ever. The homeowners association fines us if grass grows in our sidewalk cracks. Families walk the tree-lined streets to school. The kids play soccer, yes, but they also take lessons in fencing and interpretive dance. At four o'clock, our cul-de-sac is like a beehive as every family buzzes off to their activities. While we moms wait for our kids to finish math tutoring, we talk about one day moving to the middle of nowhere.

This past year, some of our neighbors stopped talking about this and started doing it. Four families pulled their kids out of school, quit their ballet and tae kwan doe lessons, and transplanted their lives to the middle of nowhere. The moms traded their minivans for homeschool curriculum. The dads now work from home or drive the two hours into downtown Houston.

Every single family that has migrated to the country has moved for the same reason: to slow down life. They are claiming their freedom from HOAs and overplanned schedules. They're choosing a life with acres of land, twenty-four-hour family time, and quiet.

Oh, and chickens. Each of these families immediately bought a flock of chickens.

My Instagram feed has changed from pictures of ballet recitals and belt testings to pictures of our free-range family friends. Their kids are learning about compost and how to raise baby chicks. The moms are relearning geometry for homeschooling, and the dads are learning how to mow the grass again. It's all extremely idyllic.

Last month we visited dear friends who had just moved to twenty acres in a nearby town of two thousand people. We fed carrots to their horse, held their squawking chickens, and admired the attic space they had remodeled into a homeschool classroom. At the end of the night, we listened to the cicadas from front-porch rockers while the kids fished in the pond. The conversation was comfortable, the pace was slow, and everyone breathed more deeply.

I wanted this life. No sidewalks, no HOA telling me I can't park in my street, no more life ruled by tardy bells and fast-food lines. No rushing. Our kids needed to play hide-and-seek without streetlights and to relax in the peace that comes from an absolutely silent country night. They needed to learn their place in the universe by staring up at an enormous starry sky.

With the picture of our family in this life lodged in my brain, I started looking at property for sale. We could sell our house for enough to buy a big chunk of land right in the middle of nothing. Now, how could I get my hands on a flock of chickens?

I gathered my evidence and presented my case to Mike. It was financially feasible to move within the year. Yes, he would have a long commute, but he could work from home more too. And yes, it would be tricky to homeschool the kids while trying to write, but I could manage. After all, I had loved being a teacher. This wasn't just a One Day dream—this could actually be our lives!

Every night Mike listened to my plans. Yes, he agreed, we could probably afford the property. And yes, he did like renovating houses. Of course, I could homeschool the kids and we would save money on tuition. He could even find a way to work from home a few days a week.

"But is this what you want?" he asked. "Do you really want to move away from our church and friends and life? Do you really want to give up your career? Do you really want to pull our kids out of the school we love so much?"

Yes. That was easy. Our family time was too fragmented. Our lives were too cluttered. I wanted to get off the racetrack and savor life. I wanted what everyone else was getting.

Then one night, I looked at him and asked the question I had been avoiding. "Is this what *you* want?"

"No," Mike answered. "Not one bit."

"What? But we're too busy now. The kids are worn out. *You're* the one who says we need to let them be kids. We both believe we have too much going on."

He put his arms around me. "Then let's quit some of it. We don't really care about Boy Scouts or swim team. And I don't think the kids do either. Let's chill out with the huge science projects. Let's not stress out about spelling tests. Let's show the kids how to be content."

Being content with my life right now sounded like regression. I gave the argument of every middle schooler and every tiger mom: "But it's making all those other people so happy! What if we're missing out?"

"Maybe a move to the country is right for them. But God is clearly giving us lots of things that are right for us where we are now. And they have nothing to do with homeschooling our kids. I love my job. You love your work. Our kids love their school. God has given us a beautiful life. Right here."

Moments like this are the sharp point of coveting that poke at my pride.

None of us wants to hear that the One Day Goal for everyone else might not work for us. We engineer our lives for progress, for upward mobility, for getting what everyone else wants. I hated the idea that God might have another plan for me. And I *really* hated the idea of being obedient to this plan.

Following the Ninth Commandment means not working for the One Day Goals of our neighbors or what your best friend tells you success is. Following the Ninth Commandment means trusting that God is giving you unique goals that will look very different from anyone else's. The path on which God takes you might be a cramped apartment in the city instead of a rambling house on a farm. Or maybe it's a small, quiet job instead of a big career. He might not take you on the path of glory but on the path of service. He may not lead you down the path of wealth but on the path of humbleness. He may not take you on the path of power but along the path of an encourager.

In the Body of Christ, you might be a foot instead of a hand, or an ear instead of an eye, but the point is not how your life is different from your friends' lives; the very important point is how we are united.

Your sister might have the gift of teaching, and you might have the gift of leading, but those gifts are from the same Spirit. Your best friend might serve from a seaside cottage and you from a crowded bungalow, but you are both serving the same Lord.

Your plans, your purpose, your gifts, your identity, your value, and your life are rooted in Jesus, God's most important gift. We are one, all adopted through His sacrifice on the cross.

Celebrate the gifts God has given you. Serve in complete confidence that you are the redeemed child of a Father who has magnificent plans for your life . . . plans right in your own backyard.

YOUR STORY/GOD'S STORY

1. Have you also adopted someone else's dream as your own? Have you abandoned your own goals to accomplish someone else's? Tell your story about a time you've found someone else's yard to be much greener than your own.

2. We all know a person who always wants what she can't have. This kind of person can be so exhausting—especially if you are that person, the one who is never satisfied. In Ecclesiastes, Solomon tells about a man who constantly complains. Read Ecclesiastes 4:4–8, and talk about how vanity makes us unhappy.

3. Coveting is a combination of lust and greed. These sins are low-grade fevers, but coveting is a blinding migraine. When you covet, you want something specific: your neighbor's house, her job, or his car. Talk about why God is so specific about what we should not covet.

4. Read Psalm 104 and discuss the ways God provides for us. As Creator, God has not only given us everything we need for our daily lives, but He's also given us our most personal blessings, like this exact family, home, and lifestyle. Talk about how seeing your blessings can act as a numbing shot to your envy.

5. God calls us to help our neighbors however we can. Whom do you know who needs your service in her life right now? Any ideas about how you could help her? How has God gifted you with specific gifts to serve others?

PRAY . . .

Heavenly Father, You know me completely and call me into specific service to the world. So often I get distracted from Your voice and lose my way. Lord, help me hear You. Keep calling me back to Your Son, the Good Shepherd. In His redeeming name. Amen.

Don't Covet Your Neighbor's Relations

"You shall not covet your neighbor's wife, or his male servant, or his female servant, or his ox, or his donkey, or anything that is your neighbor's."

—God in Exodus 20:17

"Woe to you, scribes and Pharisees, hypocrites! For you are like whitewashed tombs, which outwardly appear beautiful, but within are full of dead people's bones and all uncleanness. So you also outwardly appear righteous to others, but within you are full of hypocrisy and lawlessness.

—Jesus in Matthew 23:27–28

HERE WE ARE AT THE LAST COMMANDMENT, where God—literally—gets to the heart of all the Commandments. Or more accurately, He gets to our hearts.

Actually, God is always kind of obsessed with your heart. He mentions the heart more than a thousand times in the Bible. Over and over, He says He doesn't want the picture-perfect smile you show the world because He knows you better than that. He cares about your heart, about who you are, about your most intimate, personal self.

This makes God's love different from any other. As you've probably discovered, most people don't want to mess with your most intimate, personal self. Think of a time when your heart has been broken, like after someone you love dies. Your friends—and even your husband—are sympathetic and allow you ample time for grief. But if you don't get past it, they may eventually run out of patience with you. Their urgent, prodding message is "I'm sorry about your struggles; now, please get back to who I need you to be."

Here's the good news: your personal, intimate self is the part of you that matters most to God. He's not after a bunch of scrubbed-up, perfect kids who are hiding hearts sick with envy and sadness. God wants to change our hearts, which means He wants to change our desires. He wants us to crave the life He offers us through Jesus instead of settling for what we can get our hands on in this world.

Changing our hearts is the message of all the Commandments; it's the message of the whole Bible. I wonder if this is why God gives us this commandment last. In the Tenth Commandment, He says, "Instead of wanting the things your neighbor has, want the true peace I give you through Jesus. Instead of wanting more stuff, want more grace, more mercy, more of Me."

As we end this study, think about your heart. Would you be okay with the Holy Spirit transforming you so you crave the robe of righteousness of Jesus instead of a dead, whitewashed image?

The Tenth Commandment is God's loving command to let Christ turn your life into a new creation and your heart into one that belongs wholly to Him.

THOUGHTS ABOUT THIS COMMANDMENT

1. The explanation of this commandment is "We should fear and love God so that we do not entice or force away our neighbor's wife, workers, or animals, or turn them against him, but urge them to stay and do their duty." As we talk about this commandment, we'll look at how we should keep our eyes on our own prizes. We will also talk about how we can help other women keep their prizes. What are your thoughts before we start this commandment?

2. Look again at Luther's explanation of the Tenth Commandment. How does this look in the twenty-first century? Talk about whether we covet more or less or in exactly the same ways as humans always have.

Dying on the Inside

"Woe to you, scribes and Pharisees, hypocrites! For you clean the outside of the cup and the plate, but inside they are full of greed and self-indulgence. You blind Pharisee! First clean the inside of the cup and the plate, that the outside also may be clean."

—Jesus in Matthew 23:25–26

No one is ever really ready for a dog.

You think you are, but you can't imagine the bolt-upright-in-bed terror you'll feel when your new puppy enthusiastically guards against the evil snow at three in the morning. You can't prepare yourself for how much your dog will stink when he finds a dead rat and covers his fur in its stink.

But these are nothing compared with the two hardest parts of dog ownership: trying to decide how long your old dog should live, and the incredible pain of letting her go.

Seventeen years ago, when Mike and I had been married about one hot minute, we adopted a cocker spaniel puppy, Maddie. She was a wispy blur of white cotton fur and energy. For thousands of hours, while I wrote, she stretched her body over my bare feet. Every time I stood, she stood, always trotting behind me, always hopeful that I was getting up to give her a treat.

When we had four kids in five years, Maddie became their dog. She slept by their cribs and licked spit-up off their chins. She barked at crawling toddlers and snuggled with scared kids. She guarded our family from the UPS guy and the collie across the street. When the kids were napping and every visitor ignored the Please Don't Ring the Bell note, Maddie barked like she had distemper.

She traveled to the Midwest on about thirty family road trips, reigning as the sentinel guard dog from my lap and protecting us from motorcycles and tollbooth workers. Once, during an emergency diaper change on I-35, she escaped and ran across eight lanes of traffic—and then miraculously ran right back into our minivan.

If Maddie had been hit during her little joy run, it would have broken our hearts. Instead, our family had to deal with a slower, longer heartbreak.

When Maddie turned twelve, she started to slow down. She slept more and more, lost her hearing and her sight, stopped barking, and didn't go up the stairs. We started to prepare ourselves for her death. We adopted Manny, a retired racing greyhound, to fill the hole Maddie would leave.

But when was the right time to make such a hard decision? Every Christmas, we filled her stocking with little candy cane bones and told ourselves this would be the last year. Every road trip, we told our extended family this would be the last time they would see Maddie.

"But she looks great!" they said. "She still looks like a puppy."

This was a problem. Maddie did look great. We told our vet we were worried we wouldn't know when she was done with life. He said, "You'll know. She is ready to go when she has stopped doing everything she used to enjoy."

When she turned sixteen, we were at that point. She didn't jump up when I got her a treat, and she wanted to be left alone. She ate only a little bit every day and the bones in her skinny old body stuck out. Her teeth were breaking, and she was too old for dental surgery.

Mike and I started telling the kids that it was time to put Maddie down. This news deeply disturbed them, like we had suggested putting one of *them* down. "But she looks great!" they kept insisting. "We can't let her go yet!"

Yes, maybe so, we explained, but it would be selfish to let her live in her broken-down, bag-of-bones body. She was becoming more confused every day. She hated the diapers she had to wear. It was hard to watch her run into walls and not wake up when people stepped over her.

So we made a vet appointment for a Friday afternoon and told the kids it was time to let Maddie go. We bought her the softest, most delicious meaty feasts and fed them to her for two days straight. We took pictures of her and wrote letters to tell her she had been the best dog for sixteen long years.

But even as we showed up for our appointment, Maddie still kind of looked like her puppy self. Mike and I knew she was dying inside, and we understood it was our responsibility to let her go, but it was so hard when she looked so much like Maddie. That hour in the vet's office was one of our hardest as a family.

If you've been there with a pet, you know this. We were all crying so hard, and I was tempted to tell the kids we could take her home for another couple of months. Here's the deal, though: it didn't matter how Maddie looked on the outside; every part of her that was really *her* was gone. Her world was dark, silent, and confusing. Even if her coat was still pretty and she still looked like her puppy pictures, she was miserable.

This is the same lesson Jesus taught when He called the Pharisees white-washed tombs and clean-on-the-outside-but-dirty-on-the-inside cups and plates. It doesn't matter if you look good on the outside; the part of you that's really you is dead.

As women, we can be the worst offenders of the pretty outside/sick insides problem. In Matthew 23, Jesus delivers a tough sermon about how destructive it is to you to hide your dying inside behind a picture-perfect smile.

I don't know if Jesus' words convicted the Pharisees, but they convict me. When I read His scathing words, I'm ashamed about how much I want the world to love my outside, my image. I'm embarrassed at how much I obsess about how I look to my neighbors, but I don't think twice about my dirty soul.

When I'm at my most insecure, very afraid self, I am the first to make sure my lipstick is fresh, my clothes are new, and my hair is as rigid as my fist clutching my to-do list. Inside, I crave more attention, more approval, more money, and more validation. I crave everything this world says is valuable.

But God keeps working in my heart, exchanging my sick desires for more of Him. He is the only one who can see past my lipstick and big hair to get to my dark, gray, twisted heart. He is the only one who can change me so I stop wanting gold stars from the world.

God is the only one who can clean out your greed and jealousy, who can breathe life into those parts of your heart that have been stony for decades.

He's the only one who can cure you of coveting the life everyone around you has. He's the only one who can change us so we are no longer women who *look* like we have everything into women who *do* have everything in our Savior.

YOUR STORY/GOD'S STORY

1. Think about times when you want to make sure your outside looks perfect. What brings this out? Stress? Competition? Fear? What's your story about hiding your dying insides behind your pretty outside? What do you desire when you're in a place like this?

2. When Jesus taught about changing our hearts, He was talking about the cravings of our hearts—what we covet. What do you crave that you know is hurtful to you? How have you seen God work in your life to change your desires to want more of Him?

3. Read Jesus' sermon in Matthew 23 and the seven woes He tells will come to the scribes and Pharisees. Read His scathing words about these picture-perfect men. What's Jesus' main point? What's your takeaway from this?

4. Perhaps Jesus taught so much about faith because it can feel so hard to understand. As humans, we like what we can see and judge, but faith can be personal and mysterious. Read Matthew 15:21–28, and talk about this woman's faith. In verse 23, Jesus' disciples want Him to get rid of this strange Canaanite woman who is following them. But Jesus doesn't do that. What do His actions teach us about faith?

5. Luther says that to obey this commandment, "we should fear and love God." What does the word *fear* mean here? We know God wants to change our hearts. What kind of fear does He want us to have?

PRAY . . .

Lord, You have redeemed me and shown me my true value. I easily forget that and chase what will make me look good to the world. Clean my heart from my vanity and fill it with Your Spirit so I can recognize Jesus as my Savior. In His redeeming name. Amen.

Identical Notes
to Fraternal Twins

Everyone also to whom God has given wealth and possessions and power to enjoy them, and to accept his lot and rejoice in his toil—this is the gift of God.

—Solomon in Ecclesiastes 5:19

OUR TWINS, SAM AND ELISABETH, ARE EIGHT YEARS OLD. They have reached every single milestone in their young lives by watching the other one. For twins, crawling, walking, potty training, bike riding, name writing, and shoelace tying is a competition against the sibling.

Even today, our twins still watch each other like Olympic competitors. *What did he get on the spelling test? What was her time on the breaststroke?* Parents of twins accept this constant competition as much as we accept the extreme loyalty twins feel toward each other.

Competition is a fantastic tool to get them to finish their homework, but it quickly gets out of control. Twins—at least our twins—are always defining themselves by the other one. As a mom, I hate when they find their value in what they don't have—especially if that feeling is coming only because of what the eight-year-old next to him or her *does* have.

I wrote these identical letters to our twins to try to teach them exactly what God is trying to teach you and me: You, dear one, are exactly you for a reason. Live your story and not the one I have given your sister (or brother).

DEAR SAM,
When God made you, He knitted you together with one-of-a-kind gifts.

He created you with the rare need to be a defender of the oppressed. Suffering makes you angry, Sam. You cry when you see a homeless man on the side of the highway. If this man also has a dog, you beg me to invite both of them into our air-conditioned car.

The flip side of this deep sensitivity to others' hurting is your uncanny understanding of what makes people laugh. Even strangers love your deep, dry jokes. Your Sunday School teacher seeks you out to trade riddles with you. You are eight years old, and you have an adult's sharp sense of humor.

Because you are so insightful, you can be particularly hard on yourself. Your skin is thin, and you don't want to be different. If you knock over your glass of lemonade, you wail with shame. I know why you're crying, sweetheart. You want thicker skin, a stonier heart, and armor against the world's watching eyes.

It bothers you that your twin sister doesn't need approval like you do. How can she ignore an audience? This helps her win at swim races and at school. What is her gift that makes life so much easier for her? And why doesn't God share some of that gift with you?

I don't know why God creates us the way He does, but I can tell you His design is really intentional. Wishing you could be as focused as your sister is as useless as wishing God had given you green eyes instead of brown. You got brown for a reason—the same reason God gave you every single habit and every single gift and every single struggle.

Here is the secret: accept every part of the way God has created you, and understand He loves you as His own unique, dear child. Through your Baptism, He has claimed you to be His, wholly and completely.

God has a plan for you as unique as your fingerprints.

And His plan, dear one, will end with eternal life with Him.

LOVE, MOMMY

DEAR ELISABETH,

When God made you, He knitted you together with one-of-a-kind gifts. He created you to be the go-getter, with the discipline that would make German engineers weep with appreciation. You broke your nail-biting habit in one day through your sheer will of not disappointing yourself.

The flip side of your discipline is your expectation that everyone else will also do the right thing. Through your beautiful green eyes, life is only black-and-white. Cursing, bullying, disrespect, and stealing are always sins that should be punished completely. When you read that God said to tell your world about Him, you adopted that as your life mission. And now, when you meet a woman in a burka, you tell her Jesus died for her sins. Wow. This is passion, sweetheart.

Because you are so passionate, Elisabeth, you are particularly frustrated with the gray areas of life. Your expectations for yourself and everyone else are so high, those who don't have the same dedication as you (or those of us who chew potato chips too loudly) drive you to tears.

It bothers you that your brother doesn't struggle in the same ways you do. You wonder how your twin can joke so much. How can he be so patient, so laid-back with other people? Why has God made life so much easier for him? And why doesn't He share some of that gift with you?

I don't know why God creates us the way He does, but I can tell you it's a really intentional design. Wishing you could be as funny as your brother is as useless as wishing God had given you red hair instead of blond. You got blond for a reason, the same reason God gave you every single habit and every single gift and every struggle.

Here is the secret: accept every part of the way God has created you, and understand He loves you as His own unique, dear child. Through your Baptism, He has claimed you to be His, wholly and completely.

God has a plan for you as unique as your fingerprints.

And His plan, dear one, will end with eternal life with Him.

LOVE, MOMMY

YOUR STORY/GOD'S STORY

1. Tell your story about one woman whose life you have coveted for a very long time. Maybe it's your sister, your cousin, your best friend, or your frenemy. Is it someone close to you? What damage has this coveting caused? How has not having what she has formed your view of yourself?

2. God calls each one of us to a vocation; that is, a specific job we do in our community. Even when you're driving your kids to soccer, teaching a kindergarten class, or managing a team of accountants, you are serving the Lord by serving His people. Read 1 Corinthians 12:14–26, and talk about the roles you play in your community. How do your unique gifts help others?

3. Talk about Ephesians 4:11–16. Paul describes what a firm identity in Christ looks like. We work side by side, according to our gifts, to build up the Body of Christ. How is this picture of spiritual unity radically different from the way we live when we covet what God has given others?

4. Our God is sovereign, which means your story is not an accident. Your life has unfolded in this place, with this family, in this order, for a reason. Read Romans 9:19–21, and talk about the ways God has molded your life for honorable use in His kingdom.

5. In Luther's explanation of this commandment, he says that if we fear and love God, we will not want to turn people against one another. Discuss how this shows coveting as a heart issue. When the Holy Spirit helps you trust God, you can see your relations are exactly yours for a reason. Where do you need this refinement in your life?

PRAY . . .

Heavenly Father, thank You for the blessings of friends and family. Forgive me when I corrupt those friendships with jealousy. Replace my envy and coveting with love and generosity. Help me to follow the perfect example of my friend, Jesus. Amen.

Something's
(Not)
in the Water

But, as it is written, "What no eye has seen, nor ear heard, nor the heart of man imagined, . . . God has prepared for those who love Him."

—Paul in 1 Corinthians 2:9

IF THERE'S ONE AREA OF OUR LIVES AS WOMEN that causes us extreme joy and pain, it's our fertility. When it comes to planning our families, God's timing is almost never what we expect, and not getting what you want when you want it always adds up to serious coveting. At least that's how it worked for me.

I wanted a baby so much my arms ached for the weight of it. For years, I had plotted my life around this one role, around the big crescendo that motherhood would be in my life story. I had traveled everywhere I wanted to go, and I had climbed the career ladder as high as I had planned; now I wanted a family. Now I wanted to be someone's mother. Negative pregnancy tests always came with the double gut-punch of shame and helplessness. Every month, it felt like God was saying I wasn't good enough to be a mom, and there was not one thing I could do about that.

While I was constantly daydreaming about holding my own sweet-smelling newborn, every one of my friends got pregnant. They shared their good news shyly and with apologies. Although I was so excited for them, if I'm honest, their good news poked right at my bruises.

For a couple of years, it seems, I was invited to at least one baby shower a month. Sitting flat-stomached at a baby shower, surrounded by new moms, feels a lot like getting blackballed from a sorority.

The only thing more prevalent than pregnant women during this season was the advice that I would one day have the family God wanted me to have. *Just relax! Stop worrying about it, and it will happen!*

Every woman had the same story about almost giving up trying for a baby— and then getting a positive pregnancy test. These stories lose their effectiveness after the fifteenth time you hear them. They seem as mythical as Santa Claus must seem to a girl with no Christmas gifts. I didn't want their stories or promises; I wanted a baby of my own.

Eventually, at the exact right time, God gave us four kids of our own. After that first positive pregnancy test, my life became a flurry of maternity clothes, diapers, teething toddlers, and tiring, blissful motherhood.

Truly, I had stopped believing I would ever have kids. But then, suddenly, everything changed, and the babies were here. Just like all those other women had said it would happen.

God had this family planned for me the whole time. My envy or worry or doubt did not grow a single one of these babies or even a single hair on their heads.

The miracles had been up to God the whole time. While I was pouting about the gifts He was giving my friends, I couldn't see the pile of presents wrapped under the tree for me.

Of course, not every woman wants to be a mother, and God doesn't intend every woman to become a mother. God gives each one of us different vocations, unique paths, and our very own stories. But the beauty in these stories is that through God's grace and His Son, Jesus, every one of our stories ends with eternal life.

Trusting God means knowing He will give us—or not give us—exactly what we need. Trusting God means believing He will shine enough light for your next step, and this will turn out to be enough light for your whole, incredible life.

YOUR STORY/GOD'S STORY

1. If you're a mom, tell your fertility story. Did you ask God for kids long before He gave them to you? Or did He surprise you with a baby before you felt ready? What's your testimony about this? How can you see now that this was the exact right moment for you to start motherhood? If you're not a mom, talk about how you see this as part of your vocation and God's plan for you.

2. Look at Exodus 20:17 again. God lists what the Israelites might have coveted. What's your list? What have you wanted that seemed impossible for you to have?

3. Talk about the women throughout the Bible who have wanted a baby more than anything else. Other mothers teased Hannah (1 Samuel 1:1–8) and Sarah (Genesis 16:1–6) for their barrenness. Hannah and Sarah surely coveted the babies that Peninnah and Hagar had. Talk about how arrogance and jealousy often go hand in hand. Has this happened to you? Has someone flaunted their gifts from God to hurt you?

4. Often we just don't see that God *will* bless us one day in the exact way we are hoping. The Israelites complained bitterly for generations, not understanding that God had a plan to send a Savior. Read Galatians 4:4–7. God's timing to send a Savior came down to one specific moment in history. Through what ordinary way did God change the world?

5. Now talk about the explanation of this commandment: "We should fear and love God so that we do not entice or force away our neighbor's wife, workers, or animals." What do you covet so much that you might try to entice it away from someone else? What can cure your coveting?

PRAY . . .

Father God, Your timing is absolutely perfect in everything. Forgive me when I'm impatient with You, when I doubt You, or when I ignore Your wisdom. Send Your Holy Spirit to help me celebrate my own blessings, especially the blessing of Jesus. In His redeeming name. Amen.

Crumbling the Caste System

"Do not speak evil against one another, brothers. The one who speaks against a brother or judges his brother, speaks evil against the law and judges the law. But if you judge the law, you are not a doer of the law but a judge. There is only one lawgiver and judge, He who is able to save and to destroy. But who are you to judge your neighbor?"

—Jesus' brother James in James 4:11—12

For Catie's homework last night, she had to write an essay about caste systems. She researched the caste system in India that ranks families into different classes. We talked about how a lower-class woman has no power to change her position. As a proud citizen of the Land of the Free, Catie was appalled that one class of people could rank higher than another. She wrote a passionate essay telling the evils of caste systems and that one group of people is never better than another.

Sometimes, it feels like we as women have created a caste system among ourselves. Without even recognizing the damage we're doing, we glorify certain types of women and demonize others. A woman who wears jeans sized in the single digits is prized more highly than one in a double-digit size. If those jeans are expensive, she moves up a level. A woman with money is more important than one without. Higher degrees are better than high school diplomas. Happily married is better than divorced.

This mythical caste system we've created is ridiculous, especially since we never know what another woman's life is actually like. This is my cautionary tale about the lies of our caste system.

When I was in my late twenties, a publisher offered to buy my first book, an unbelievable dream I never really guessed would come true. Ever since I had picked up *Cat in the Hat* as a kindergartner, I had wanted to be a writer. After filling up three bulletin boards with rejection letters, I could not believe someone was offering me actual money for my stories.

At the time, I was a high school English and religion teacher, and I was buried in the fun, chaotic life of work. Mike was a new consultant for a software company and traveled every week. With him out of town, I threw myself into fourteen-hour days at school. Life was a hamster wheel of working, grad school, and late dinners with friends. It was fun, but I missed Mike. Weekends weren't enough time to reconnect.

So when the publisher offered me the contract, I took this as permission to step off the hamster wheel and write full time. Mike was traveling so much that Southwest Airlines had awarded us a companion pass so I could fly free with him. His company staffed him at a job in New Orleans, one of the most fascinating cities in the country. Suddenly, it seemed like everything was coming up Hergenrader.

Mike would work all day in the French Quarter, and I would write at our hotel across from his office. I had hours and hours alone in a silent room with only a computer and my own thoughts. After writing my first book during short, middle-of-the-night spurts, full days to write were an unfathomable gift.

Any writer will tell you that lots of time to think sounds lovely—until you're actually alone with your own thoughts. Having a book due should have motivated me to write like the dickens. Instead, writer's block set in.

When I couldn't seem to think enough to spell my own name, I would leave the hotel room and go for meandering walks through the beignet stands and walk-up daiquiri bars. I walked so many miles of the French Quarter, I couldn't stand it. It smelled like pee and beer, and everyone came in to party and left all their trash. Also, I was desperately lonely and envious of groups of girlfriends who stayed in my hotel, laughing and screaming through the night. I wanted to ask them to please be quiet. I had a book to write—and it was not happening.

Another miscalculation was how expensive it was for me to travel with Mike. Essentially, we were living in one of the priciest areas of the country without my income. A bottle of water cost five bucks. We couldn't afford a rental car or the fancy seafood restaurants that surrounded our hotel. I smuggled boxes of cereal from the hotel's free breakfast and ate them all day. By the time we flew home, I couldn't look at a box of Golden Grahams.

Right around this time, my alma mater named me Young Alumnus of the Year, and I had to speak at homecoming. This felt like being named Golfer of the Year when I had never picked up a club. Total fraud. I was living the life of a quintessential writer without accomplishing very much writing at all. Instead, I was depressed—and realizing that quitting my job had been a mistake.

Most of my college friends had become teachers, and they came to the homecoming festivities. We met for dinner and told about our lives. Many of them were new mothers who were struggling to balance a classroom full of kids with their own kids at home. They were living the hamster wheel of lesson plans, coaching volleyball games, and family life. They told me they envied my life, my free time with my husband, and my dream career.

They said, "I wish I were a writer," and "I wish I could travel with my husband," and "You are so lucky." My low-grade depression bloomed into a piercing pain.

"No," I told them. "I'm not making any progress on my book. I'm scared and just wander around a lot of the day, worrying. I am so lonely."

I told them the truth, that I had made a mistake when I quit my job. I wanted their full lives, their families, their purpose.

The walls of the caste system began to crumble a bit as they said their lives were hard too. We talked about this for so long that the waiter brought us menus to order a second dinner. In the end, we all agreed that life is just hard. Imagining that our better reality is just one higher rung in the caste system is silly.

Judging and ranking the lives of other women is still silly. It's still hurtful. Can we agree that placing women into levels completely ignores Christ's equalizing work on the cross? Can we admit that believing someone else's life is better than our own life causes us to covet—and that it completely ignores our Father, who is telling crazy-good, exciting stories in our lives? Can we agree that seeing ourselves as stuck completely ignores the Holy Spirit's work as transformer?

This side of heaven, God's work is never done. Instead of telling ourselves false narratives about everyone else who has everything else, let's ask God to open our eyes to what we have and to what He promises us in eternity.

Let's ask Him to help us see His creation—and the people in it—as fully flawed and fully redeemed children of King Jesus.

YOUR STORY/GOD'S STORY

1. Tell about a season in your life when you felt someone else (or a group of someone elses) coveting what you had. Did it feel accurate? Why or why not? What's the lesson here?

2. Life isn't as linear as we like to think. Even if your life is lonely now, the next season might be rich with friends. Even if you're feeling financially stretched right now, God might bless you with financial comfort. Even if you feel scared and without faith right now, God will fill your heart with trust for Him. Talk about the lies coveting tells us about life.

3. Talk about Romans 3:22–25. In what desperate way are we all alike? What does each of us need from God? Why are we so hesitant to admit we're flawed and in need of His forgiveness?

4. Look at Colossians 3:9–11. As women, we can believe in a mythical caste system that places some higher than others. Talk about how through Christ, one of us is not better than another. Why is this good news?

5. The main problem with the caste system is that when you see life as a race, you are tempted to trip those in front of you. But God is clear: He wants us to love and help our neighbors. In Luther's explanation of the commandment, he says, "urge them to stay and do their duty." How could you help others do their duty?

PRAY . . .

Father, Your grace is the great equalizer. Because of Your love, each of us is equally valuable and equally loved. Teach me to love Your grace and to rejoice in my identity as a forgiven sinner. Teach me to live in the forgiveness of Jesus. In His redeeming name. Amen.

Love Rules
Conclusion

Thank you so much for studying the Ten Commandments with me.

Who knew that these seventeen verses in Exodus, written thousands of years ago, would be so meaningful to our lives today?

Better yet, who knew every single one of these Commandments would show us how much God loves us?

And who knew that following the Ten Commandments would be so easy? Oh, wait. Just kidding about that last one.

You and I know that following God's Commandments is really hard. A life of obedience to God is like Whack-A-Mole. While God is refining one part of your heart, another part of you is out of control, spreading gossip or lusting after something He never meant for you to have.

This is our lifelong tension between sinner and saint, life on earth and life in heaven, flawed and forgiven.

This tension can feel exhausting, can't it? It seems like you are never fully sinner or saint. Or you want to be a saint, but the sinner keeps taking over. Loving God and each other better is a lifelong lesson that's impossible to perfect.

Even so, we keep trying at the Ten Commandments. Trying, failing, trying again, failing better—or worse.

But even failing is the best news in the world when we understand God's love. He picks us up when we fall down. We are so valuable to Him, He keeps showing us His amazing grace.

God's grace: this is the heart of this book, the heart of the Commandments, and the heart of our lives as fully redeemed daughters of our Father. Because of grace, Jesus kept the Commandments for us. He took on all our punishment. He went to hell—and back—for us. Out of love.

And His Love Rules All.

Let's live in that love, and let's share it with the world.

CHRISTINA

www.christinasbooks.com

Answers

Commandment One. 1. This commandment asks who or what you trust more than anything else. Perhaps it's easier for us to fear God and love Him than it is to trust Him to take care of us during the hardest seasons of our lives. **2.** Answers will vary, but women will talk about trusting in family or dear friends, career and success more than they trust in God.

1. Roots. 1. Answers will vary. **2.** Friendships can provide fun, love, encouragement, and camaraderie. Friendships that give you your security, your value, or your identity will fracture under the pressure. **3.** Answers will vary but will include that God cares for you so deeply that even the hairs on your head are numbered. He cares completely for you in the exact ways you need Him to. He wants you to put your security in Him. **4.** God provides us with His constant love, promise of eternal life, forgiveness for every sin, peace through His love, and our faith through His Word and Sacraments. **5.** Answers will vary, but women will talk about where they need God's help to have realistic expectations about their relationships.

2. Super Sam. 1. Answers will vary. **2.** Answers will vary and include we want life to unfold according to our timeline, not God's. God knows the perfect time for both birth and death. The Holy Spirit perfectly shows us God's work, but it can be so hard for us to trust it. **3.** To name a few, Sarah and Abraham often relied on their own ideas, unable to fathom the huge plan God really had for them. Joseph's life was filled with so many pitfalls that turned into blessings. God's plan to send a Savior spanned thousands of years. **4.** Answers will vary but will include that God wants you to trust Him because His plans endure forever (Ecclesiastes 3:14). We can trust God's love and perfect vision for our future as revealed in His Word. We can't know what will happen to us in the next hour or the next decade. Every one of our earthly plans might fail. But God's perfect, eternal plan for us has already been accomplished through the work of Christ Jesus. Because we are His baptized and redeemed children, we can be certain of that! **5.** Answers will vary, but women will talk about how obeying, loving, and trusting God means radical faith, the kind of faith we can have only through the power of the Holy Spirit.

3. The Beach-House God. 1. Answers will vary, but women's stories will include that the love of money plunges us to a place we don't want to be. Thanks to the work of the Holy Spirit, we crave God's eternal love more than we crave eternal things. **2.** If we only trust what we can earn or buy ourselves, our lives will become small, temporary, and limited to this disappointing life. Our intangible treasures are in heaven. They are eternal and from our Father, who loves us. God does make our faith tangible through everyday elements like water in Baptism and bread and wine in Holy Communion. **3.** Answers will vary, but most will talk about their struggle to trust money more than their heavenly Father as their true God, who will take care of them. **4.** You are a child of God. You are a light bearer to the world. You are not valuable because of what you can buy; you are valuable because Christ loved you enough to be your sacrifice. **5.** Answers will vary, but women will talk about places they specifically need God's help to keep *Him* as their true Savior, instead of money or things.

4. Mom's Superpowers. 1. Answers will vary; women will tell how, thanks to faith, we can see our weakness as a blessing that shows God's strength. **2.** We are completely dependent on God's goodness. We cannot survive independent of Him. **3.** God knows independence from Him is hell. We can't save ourselves. Earthly tools—our own intellect, hard work, and perseverance—save us as effectively as the golden calf saved the Israelites. True protection comes from God, through Christ. **4.** Answers will vary but will include that God wants our whole lives to be rooted in Him. Our service, talents, and abilities flow from our Creator, and we use them to serve Him. **5.** Answers will vary; women will talk about how they realize they are not indestructible. They deeply know their own need for a Savior, but it can be so hard to admit and live in our own weakness.

Commandment Two. 1. Answers will vary, but most women will talk about how God's name can be a powerful exclamation point to anything we say. Examples might include, "Oh, my God!"; "I swear to God!"; "God told me to do this." Any time we attach God's name to our own agenda, we take His influence to make ourselves more influential. **2.** Using the Lord's name in vain is not just a problem with our speech; it's a problem with our souls. God tells us to deny ourselves to follow Him. The words we use reveal what we worship.

5. Vine > Branches = Truth. 1. Answers will vary but should include that when we want independence from God, we devalue His strength. We misuse His name. We reduce and change God to fit our own purposes. **2.** This is absolutely the way our relationship with God works. Our egos want God to behave in the exact ways we think He should. When He doesn't, we devalue Him. But God works deeper and in ways we can't understand. He keeps inviting us to see His love. Only the Holy Spirit can help you see God's work in your life. **3.** Jesus says that His sheep hear His voice. We hear Christ's voice through following Him, reading His Word, praying, and serving Him. When we belong to Him, nothing can snatch us out of His hand. **4.** Answers will vary and include personal testimonies. **5.** Answers will vary but will include we abuse God's name when we want independence from Him and what He teaches about His name. The Holy Spirit can humble our hearts to help us fear and love God.

6. Microwaving the Sacred. 1. Answers will vary but will include that we shrink God to control Him so we can remain the authority in our own lives. **2.** If you're in a cynical season, feeling detached from God and uninspired, call on the One who inspires your faith. Ask the Holy Spirit for new eyes to see God's work in your life. God always answers this prayer with renewed faith. **3.** Answers will vary, but women will talk about how the ceremony of God's name helps us understand our relationship with Him. We are dependent on Him. He is bigger than we can understand, and that's praiseworthy. **4.** Answers will vary but will include that Mary's song of praise articulates her understanding of God's immeasurable power and love. She praises Him by saying He is holy and she is His faithful servant. **5.** Answers will vary but will include women's hopes to better use God's name to thank Him and call on Him when they're afraid or desperate.

7. Real Sunshine & the Chick-fil-A Drive-Through. 1. Answers will vary. **2.** We say we'll pray for one another, but we avoid the real encounter of coming to Jesus. We join Christian groups, but we never study the Bible or apply it to our lives. When we do this, we totally miss what we're looking for, which is the new heart the Holy Spirit offers us, thanks to Christ's sacrifice. **3.** Saying you're a Christian without living a life truly transformed by Christ is false advertising. If you call yourself a Christian but show the world an impotent, shallow example, you are using God's name in vain. God doesn't want us to do this, because He knows we need the real healing that comes from the redemptive blood of Christ. **4.** Answers will vary but will include that the Holy Spirit changes us from wanting to serve ourselves to wanting to serve God. In the parable of the sower, Jesus explains how some peoples' hearts always remain rocky. **5.** Answers will vary.

8. Our Father, Who Trademarked His Name. 1. Answers will vary but will include stories of God answering prayer immediately and miraculously and about God answering prayers over several decades. **2.** Using God's name as He instructed us to, in prayer but not in vain, reminds us that God is the true God and the only one who can truly change our lives. Using God's name in vain is our sinful attempt to rub the holiness from it. **3.** We call on God's name, confident He loves us and has chosen us to be His. We pray in Jesus' name because He is our intercessor (Hebrews 7:25). Jesus' name is our powerful reminder of our relationship with God. **4.** God commands us not to use His name to promote our own pride. That's "copyright infringement" because His name is sacred. He loves us and has the power to change our scared hearts and minds. Using His name as He tells us to helps us see that. God tells us we are valuable, we can come before Him and ask anything of Him in Jesus' name. **5.** Answers will vary but will include that the Holy Spirit urges our souls to cry out to our heavenly Father for our deepest desires.

Commandment Three. 1. Answers will vary, but women will talk about how they fall into the bad habit of prioritizing work and kids' activities over church. **2.** Answers will vary, but women will tell about times of passionate Bible study and also about cynical seasons of not caring about church or Bible study.

9. Holy Work. 1. Answers will vary but will include that the Holy Spirit inspires faith in us. Pray for God to help you want to be at church, worshiping with other believers and receiving His good gifts. **2.** Not going to church is an ancient problem, and we know this because the author of Hebrews also talks about this trend. People don't go to church for lots of reasons, including inconvenience, anger, hurt pride, believing church is irrelevant to their lives, and unbelief. All these are rooted in our own lies about what we believe about ourselves. We trust God when He says worship is an important part of our Christian lives. **3.** In the Divine Service, Jesus is right there. He is as present in church as He is in heaven. This can happen anywhere, but it happens on a weekly, predictable time at church. Go to church and be part of communion with Christ. **4.** Worship services typically include hearing God's Word, praise and prayer, receiving the Sacraments of Baptism and Holy Communion, and receiving forgiveness and absolution. **5.** Answers will vary.

10. Praise & Popularity. 1. Answers will vary. **2.** Observing a Sabbath means resting and praising God, which roots your identity in Him. We admit we are weak and need rest. We see we need God, not the other way around. **3.** Serving other people and serving ourselves will never, ever give us the value we're searching to earn from them. They can't provide it. But your value in God comes from your identity as His chosen daughter. His love, proven when He sent His Son to redeem you, was given to you in your Baptism. **4.** One day, we will rest in heaven with our Father and Savior. **5.** Answers will vary, but women will talk about wanting an increased desire to study and learn God's Word.

11. The Rhythm of Kale Chips & French Fries. 1. Answers will vary, but usually our human productivity is rooted in pride, which makes us want to accomplish more. **2.** *Holy* means set apart, or different. Sunday should look different from your other days, just like God stopped creating the universe so He could rest. The Sabbath should be the day you stop working to rest. **3.** Answers will vary but will include that God did not design us to work seven days a week, right up to the end of our energy. Exodus 23:11 is a reminder to let the land rest every seven years, just like we rest on the seventh day. **4.** Yes! Chick-fil-A is a great example of how a Sabbath looks. A day to rest and worship allows employees the perspective, rejuvenation, and fellowship with Christians they need. They return refreshed. **5.** Answers will vary but will include that resting and hearing God's Word are cyclical. God's Word changes our hearts so we crave more of Him and trust Him more. When we trust Him, we are also able to rest in Him.

12. Kicking & Screaming. 1. Answers will vary but will include we are imperfect at resting and worshiping. God forgives us and gives us more and more chances to trust that we can rest in Him. **2.** Answers will vary, but women will talk about finding a rhythm that includes work and rest. Finding your value in the work you do, instead of in your identity as God's daughter, is sinful. **3.** God is our Creator and knows what our bodies and our souls need. He tells us we need a day we can totally rest from our work. The Sabbath is part of our instruction manual for our bodies. Taking a break is exactly what we need and deeply desire; therefore, it's a gift. **4.** Answers will vary but will include that God commands rest and worship, and this is the most vital reason to go to church. **5.** Answers will vary but will include that God answers our prayers to change our habits to bring us closer to Him. Even for those who work on weekends, God calls us to find time to rest and worship Him.

Commandment Four. 1. Answers will vary, but women may talk about how obeying their parents might be the hardest. As we mature and become independent, we don't like the idea of obeying our parents. It might be easiest to love our parents but hardest to serve and obey them. **2.** Answers will vary, and women will share their family stories that range from the idyllic to the abusive. Your discussion will prepare you for your study of the commandment.

13. Family Honor & Family Armor. 1. Answers will vary. **2.** Most women will report that forgiveness is difficult. If they have forgiven their parents for their mistakes, they understand the way this changes their relationship with them so life together is possible. **3.** The relationship with your parents is perhaps your most complicated. Unlike your husband or your friends, you didn't choose your parents. Your relationship with them endures significant changes, as your dependence on them changes. Nevertheless, the Fourth Commandment tells us to honor them and recognize that they have authority over us. **4.** Relationships with your family do not have to be defined by the past. We are ambassadors for Christ now. This means God can even change generational curses! **5.** Yes. God instructs us to forgive, and we do because we love Him. Realizing that forgiving our parents is an act of love prompts us to keep showing grace in one of our most complicated relationships.

14. Knitting Lessons. 1. Answers will vary, but many women will tell stories of their family helping each other through the most painful parts of life. **2.** The reason we don't submit to authority or honor our parents is because of our pride. Humans have always been prideful, and therefore, children have always struggled to honor their parents. **3.** Answers will vary but will include that the Holy Spirit gives us the tools and tenacity we need to follow God's commands. **4.** For Adam and Eve's family, even after Cain killed Abel, God gave them the blessing of Seth, and through him, the lineage that would include Christ. In Abraham's family, God gave Sarah and Abraham Isaac, in spite of Abraham's sin of polygamy. God allowed His blessing to flow to Jacob, in spite of Rebekah's deceitfulness. God blessed Jacob with twelve sons, in spite of his sin of polygamy and favoritism. At the end of Genesis, Joseph and his brothers reunite, even though his brothers had sinned against him. **5.** Answers will vary.

15. You Will (Probably) Turn into Your Mother. 1. Answers will vary but will include that through families, especially mother-daughter relationships, we learn our most important lessons. As an honorable mom, you have the unique opportunity to share God's love with your kids. **2.** Answers will vary but will include women's stories about seasons in their lives when they helped their kids find their identity in places other than God, like in the security of money, in co-dependent relationships, and in the misguided loyalty to family over God. These hurtful lessons did not grow the kind of family God intended. **3.** Christ lives in you and gives you the power to live an honorable life. God wants you to trust that His forgiveness covers a multitude of sins. **4.** God redeemed Timothy's story. The Holy Spirit helped the seeds of faith grow in Timothy's heart so he could share the exciting news of Christ with the world. God can work through any family situation to bring His children to Him. **5.** Answers will vary but will include that the most honorable part of your job as mother is sharing the Good News of Christ's sacrifice with your kids.

16. Salute the Uniform. 1. Answers will vary, but the most important part of honoring your parents' place in you life is to understand you can never change their sinful habits; only God can. You can never punish them; only God can.

"Saluting the uniform" might mean limiting the time you spend with them and establishing boundaries about how much influence they have on you and your kids. **2.** Answers will vary, but most women will talk about how honoring our parents can be so difficult. As humans, we're better at liking. The ability to honor your parents comes from God and includes respecting their important place in your life. **3.** Yes, sin damages our relationships. But as children of our heavenly Father, we know our identity is so much richer than a graveyard of damaged relationships. We are clay jars of the living, breathing Christ. Our relationships live in this light. **4.** Answers will vary, but most women will talk about how they hope to show the fruit of the Spirit in their relationship with their parents. **5.** Answers will vary but will include that it's only with the help of the Holy Spirit that we can forgive and honor our sinful parents.

Commandment Five. 1. Answers will vary, but women will talk about how we use our words, our energy, our wills, our time to hurt other women's reputations, their feelings, and their own walk with God. **2.** Answers will vary, but women will tell stories about how difficult it is to like those who have hurt us or whom we don't trust. Let this conversation prime your group for a deeper discussion of this commandment.

17. Sick Revenge. 1. Answers will vary. **2.** God tells us we reap what we sow. If the Holy Spirit rules our souls, our lives are filled with fruit of the Spirit. If our ego and Satan rule our souls, our lives are filled with temporary victory that eventually ends in pain. Kevin missed out on a true life with his daughter, the deep connection that comes with years of marriage, and God's blessings that come with following His Commandments. Lindy's hate fueled the sinful, dark part of her soul. **3.** When you refuse to forgive, you might find it hard to sleep, eat, or like yourself very much. Also, when you see the world through hate-filled glasses, you miss the other promises and blessings from God in your life. **4.** Yes, forgiveness is a miracle. Forgiveness is from God, and we are made in His image. Because of His love, we can share forgiveness with the world. **5.** God tells us to forgive one another, just as He forgives us. Forgiveness is God's gift to us, thanks to Christ's sacrifice on the cross. It serves as the balm that makes life together enjoyable rather than painful.

18. Everyone Has a Mother-in-Law Story. 1. Answers will vary but will include women's stories about misunderstandings, unhealthy relationships, and other in-law drama. Relationships rooted in Christ are covered with forgiveness and the fruit of the Spirit. **2.** Answers will vary but will include stories of women believing lies Satan tells us when we feel angry or hurt. **3.** Ruth left her country of Moab, and its pagan gods, to follow Naomi back to Bethlehem and worship her God, the God of the Israelites. Even in the season of pain and death, God brought Ruth close to Him, and she clung to Naomi and to God. Orpah went back to her pagan people, which could have been Ruth's choice too. **4.** When the Holy Spirit rules our lives, we see the fruit of this in how we treat people. When we rule our lives with our own selfishness, we see Satan's work of hatred and selfishness in our lives. **5.** Answers will vary.

19. Spiritual Antibiotics. 1. Answers will vary but should include that God shows us His love in millions of ways every day. Anger is not believing that God will take care of you. **2.** Answers will vary but will include that God always gives us security and love, even when we're faced with inflammatory situations. He loves when we pray and tell Him what we need. **3.** Bless those who persecute you. Rejoice with those who rejoice, and weep with those who weep. Instead of being prideful, show love to those who need it. God wants you to live in peace with everyone. **4.** Before you go to the altar with a sacrifice for God, Jesus tells us to make peace with others. Forgiveness is best for us, and Jesus doesn't want us to ignore that and choose self-righteousness. He wants our whole hearts in His love and light. **5.** Answers will vary.

20. The African Children's Choir. 1. Answers will vary. **2.** Answers will vary. **3.** God has given us much, and He commands us to help others. As Jesus taught, those who are dying because they don't have food, water, and shelter are our responsibility. God's system for helping those poorer than we are is the hands, feet, and hearts of those of us who are able and who love the Lord. **4.** Feeding the hungry is about showing love. By feeding the thousands, Jesus showed He loved and took care of them. When we feed the hungry, we also have the chance to show Jesus' love to the multitudes and to build a relationship with them. **5.** Answers will vary.

Commandment Six. 1. Sex should only be part of marriage. A pure life means saving this powerful, sacred connection for only your husband. In other words, a pure life means no living together or sex until marriage. **2.** When you don't love and honor your husband with your words and actions, you're violating the sacred relationship God has established in marriage. We do this when we let pride and impatience creep into our relationships. As you read the following stories, think about your own marriage and what you can ask God to do to help you better love and honor your husband.

21. Pride Cometh before the Affair. 1. Answers will vary, but most women will say that when you choose independence from your husband, you push away true intimacy and the marriage God wants you to have. **2.** Answers will vary but will include that living as one flesh means sacrifices and submissions. This is hard for all of us. We always choose self over submission. We need God to help us choose unity over independence. **3.** Answers will vary but will include that Jesus says to constantly forgive. Marriage, a life forever in true intimacy, means real reconciliation with your husband over and over again. **4.** Bathsheba became his wife and David loved their new son, Solomon. The couple moved past the sin at the start of their marriage for a lifelong union with each other. **5.** Answers will vary but will include that love and honor mean self-sacrifice, which is the opposite of pride.

22. The Endorphins Will Carry You. 1. Answers will vary, but most women will talk about how short bursts of emotion don't deliver like real training. Slow and steady perseverance comes from commitment, and it's what we need in marriage. **2.** Answers will vary but will include that God commands marriage to be a lifetime commitment during bad times as well as good. To have an affair during the tough seasons would be to miss the deeper love right around the corner. **3.** Living as a new creation means we identify ourselves in our Baptism (as God's children) instead of in our sin. Over the lifetime of our marriages, the Holy Spirit is constantly teaching us how to trust and forgive each other. **4.** The family is at the core of God's plan for His creation. God chose His people through a married couple (Abraham and Sarah). He also sent His Son through a family (Mary and Joseph). Marriage matters to God. It's through this human covenant that He gives His unique blessings. **5.** God institutes marriage as His design for families. He wants us to stay married forever. This means that loving and honoring your husband honors God and His institution.

23. Depressing Weddings. 1. Answers will vary but will include divorce stories, most caused when a husband and wife stop connecting spiritually, emotionally, and physically. **2.** Answers will vary, but women who have been divorced will say it's very, very painful. God doesn't want us to separate what He's joined together. **3.** In a lifelong marriage, there must be the forgiveness that God gives us through our Savior, Jesus. As in all the Commandments, God tells us to forgive others as He forgives us. **4.** Like a three-legged race, your husband's faith life is tied to yours. Serving and loving God together means praying for your husband when he stumbles and meeting his stride when he leads you to a closer walk with God. **5.** Answers will vary but will include that God wants you to learn the lessons of self-sacrifice and grace. Pray for ways to show forgiveness to your husband.

24. A Letter to My Eleven-Year-Old Daughter. 1. Answers will vary, but most women will say they wish they had realized that sex before marriage leads to regrets later in life. **2.** God's definition of adultery is different from society's. People who live together don't see this as adultery because they don't understand that God's design for a lifelong commitment means having sex only within the covenant of marriage. **3.** "Joseph, being a just man and unwilling to put her to shame, resolved to divorce her quietly" (Matthew 1:19). Women found guilty of adultery could be stoned. Birth control and abortion have made sex outside of marriage much, much more common and accepted. However, medical advancements don't consider the emotional turmoil teenagers experience when they have sex before they're married. **4.** Answers will vary but will include that God always gives us free will because He wants us to experience the deeper love that comes with choosing Him. When you sacrifice your appetites to wait until marriage to have sex, you give your spouse the most precious wedding present ever. **5.** Answers will vary but will include that purity may seem impossible during the dating years, but as we get older, we realize how important it is. In this commandment we see God's love for us as He protects us from the hurts that come with premarital sex.

Commandment Seven. 1. Answers will vary but will include that our modern world is absolutely covered in this kind of "how to get something for nothing" mentality. You only need to open your email or read today's headlines to see how the world tries to get something for nothing. **2.** It is never our instinct to love others more than we love ourselves. But this is exactly how Jesus loves us. He sacrificed everything to give us eternal life. He calls us to also sacrifice for others.

25. Shopping & Prozac. 1. Answers will vary. **2.** Answers will vary but will include that leaning on money for security is one of our greatest temptations. God knew we would struggle with greed and that it would lead to sins like stealing and stockpiling. Jesus wants us to choose the better identity and the free grace He offers to us through His perfect life and sacrifice. **3.** The love of money causes all kinds of evil; the most obvious is stealing. God protects us from this by teaching us, over and over, to come to Him for fulfillment instead of looking to money. **4.** Women will say that a greedy person isn't inherently trustworthy, but a person who serves God lives a life in the Spirit. Their life will show the fruit of the spirit: kindness, goodness, faithfulness, and self-control. **5.** Answers will vary but will include that God wants us to feel content with our own gifts. He wants us to help our neighbor keep her gifts. He wants to fill our hearts with His love so we can feel peace, which is the opposite of greed.

26. Sisters & Stealing. 1. Answers will vary but will include that pride tells us we deserve and need more than others do and that stealing is okay. **2.** God is the God of every single person. He loves and protects each of us equally. When we take something from another person, we not only sin with greed, but we also sin by hurting others and taking that person's gifts from them. **3.** Answers will vary but will include that leaning on money for security is one of our greatest temptations. Spiritual blessings are eternal. **4.** God cares for us constantly, completely, and daily. Because He provides exactly what we need, when we need it, insecurity and greed are lies and sins. God wants His children to know the security of believing we are valued more than any of His other creations. **5.** Answers will vary.

27. Rise Up & Whine! 1. Answers will vary and will include women's testimonies of tithing and giving. Women will talk about how hard it can be to give more than we think we can spare, but how God always provides exactly the right gifts for us. **2.** Answers will vary, but women will talk about how they give their time and their talents besides their treasures. **3.** God commands us to give cheerfully because this helps us understand what money can do and what it cannot do. It cannot provide happiness, so giving away our money lets us see our joy is in the Lord and not tied to our stuff. **4.** The Holy Spirit continues to plant the seed of faith in our hearts. Yes, money and possessions and the world's message of greed have a foothold in our soul, but faith from the Holy Spirit falls anew and can rid this lie from our hearts. **5.** Answers will vary but will include that the Holy Spirit nudges us to open our hearts and give more of our blessings to help others.

28. House Hunters. 1. Answers will vary and will include women's testimonies about how God always gives us the exact gifts we need. We don't have to scheme or stockpile; He takes care of every single need. **2.** Answers will vary, but most women will tell stories about how they feel like they deserve their children/money/time/friends. This entitlement makes us scheme to hold on to what we've "earned." Everything good is a gift from God, and when we can see this, we understand the right relationship with Him as provider. **3.** Answers will vary but will include that it's when we feel trapped that we find ourselves scheming to get what's not ours. We can pray for faith that God will take care of us. **4.** Even though we love the earthly blessings God gives us, they are nothing compared with the fantastic life we will have with our Savior in heaven. **5.** Answers will vary but will include that our hope is in the Lord. He doesn't want us to scheme because this damages others and wrongly teaches us that we can take care of ourselves.

Commandment Eight. 1. Yes. We still use our words to hurt others. We defame in Internet comments, we slander in text messages, we betray through conversations. Even five hundred years after Martin Luther explained this commandment, we still struggle with the same sins. **2.** Answers will vary, but women will tell stories about slanting situations to defame others, especially the women they struggle to like.

29. Beat Up by Gossip. 1. Answers will vary, but women will tell stories about how it feels for a group to gossip about them. **2.** Answers will vary, but most women will say that not gossiping would help stop the spread of lies. Following this commandment also teaches us self-control, kindness, and obedience. **3.** Hate corrupts our soul and pushes out God's Word. Gossip isn't just meaningless chatter—it's chatter with malicious intent. **4.** Jesus tells us to treat others like we would like to be treated. No one wants to be judged and exploited for her mistakes. That's the lesson in the Eighth Commandment, to treat stories about other women the way we wish women would treat stories about us. **5.** Answers will vary but will include that the Holy Spirit shows us ways to use our words to help others.

30. The Ugly Stepchild of Church Missions. 1. Answers will vary. **2.** Answers will vary but will include that telling ourselves we are victims completely ignores God's love and grace and plans for our lives. **3.** Jesus talked directly to those who needed love, those who persecuted Him, and those who lied to Him. Jesus didn't passively aggressively tell His disciples what He thought of the Pharisees—He told the Pharisees. **4.** Gossip is often our attempt to manipulate and control other people's perceptions. We spread gossip to redefine another person, according to who we need them to be for our convenience. **5.** Answers will vary but will include that we slander and betray when we want to seem more important or better than other women. You can pray for the Holy Spirit to change your heart to truly love your neighbor as yourself.

31. Camp Love Triangles. 1. Answers will vary, but most women will talk about how their frustration blinded them at the time so they couldn't see the other person's hurt or hope. God wants to tell huge, wonderful stories of grace in our lives. Gossip paints lies over His stories. **2.** Answers will vary but will include that the difference between verbally processing and gossiping has much to do with the intent of the woman who's telling the story. **3.** We gossip for lots of reasons, including boredom, the need to control, fear, anger, and insecurity. Yes, idle time does go along with gossiping. Sometimes we invent drama by talking about someone we don't like. **4.** Jesus helped Martha move to His perspective. Perhaps this is the best thing we can do for a woman who needs to tell her story. Listen and then help her see love in her situation. **5.** Answers will vary.

32. A Manifesto to Stop All the Lying. 1. Answers will vary, but we usually exaggerate and compete with those women who seem to have everything figured out. In a relationship where you can't tell the truth, you're not connecting in an honest, real way. It's probably not a great relationship. **2.** Answers will vary, but most women will tell stories about how they lie about drinking too much, spending too much, feeling alone or afraid, and yelling at their families. God wants us to change by helping us find the root of our problems and confessing the sins there. After we're forgiven, He wants us to live in the light of His truth. **3.** Answers will vary, but women will tell stories about telling lies to fit into this world. Crying out to God with the absolute truth is exactly the freedom our souls need, and these kinds of prayers help us, even before God answers the prayer. **4.** When we honestly tell where we're messing up, we realize our desperate need for a Savior. This is why we have Confession and Absolution in prayer, in church, and in our relationship with Christ. **5.** Answers will vary but will include that when the Holy Spirit helps us see our true identity in Christ, we can live honestly in that identity.

Commandment Nine. 1. Answers will vary but will include that if you're content with what God's given you, you won't covet. If you're full of gratitude for your own gifts, talents, and house, you won't lust after what the woman next to you has. **2.** The Ninth Commandment isn't only about our hearts but about our actions that flow out of our hearts. When you understand your gifts from God, who loves you, you are not only satisfied with your own gifts, but you also want to help others keep the gifts God has given them.

33. The Lie of the Pie. 1. Answers will vary. **2.** Answers will vary, but women will say we miss out when we fail to live generously with one another and show one another grace. We can absolutely be like the older brother in the parable, seeing our Father's generosity like a finite pie and fighting for what we deserve. God is the Father throwing a party, and He wants all His children to celebrate His abundance. **3.** God gives us blessings and tells us to share. Instead of coveting or being afraid of running out, give generously to your community. God will keep providing. **4.** Coveting is the start of all kinds of selfish choices. In Deuteronomy 15:10, we understand that God loves when we give, and He will always provide for us. **5.** Answers will vary.

34. Instagram & Chocolate Cake Pops. 1. Answers will vary but will include that social media can make women crave other people's lives and validation from the world. **2.** Answers will vary, but women will talk about the blessings God has given them. We don't need more from God; we need the eyes to see what He's already given us. To help us notice His gifts, we can say prayers of thanksgiving. Keeping a gratitude journal might also help. **3.** Attention, including "likes" on social media, fills up your ego. Your ego makes you believe that the good parts of your life are a result of your excellent taste and hard work. Really, these are all gifts from God. **4.** Answers will vary but will include that Facebook, Instagram, and YouTube could be incredible ways to share the message of Jesus Christ with the lost. **5.** Answers will vary.

35. Shiny Gold Glitter Dust. 1. Answers will vary, but most women will tell stories about finding their value in how they relate to the other women in their lives, rather than in their status as God's child. **2.** The problem with finding value in an ever-changing view of this world is that you never truly feel loved. More than anything, God wants us to know we are His cherished children whom He loved enough to send His Son to save. **3.** Answers will vary, but women will share stories about finding their value in money and their own hard work. But knowing you are completely loved by your Father and Savior fills you with security. We can be confident in our lives. The word *confident* means "living with faith." **4.** Answers will vary, but women will talk about the unique gifts God has given each one of them. God has equipped each of us to share His love with the world. Through the power of Jesus, we can share our identity in God with those who need to see it. **5.** Answers will vary but will include that the Holy Spirit is the only one who can change our hearts so we see our homes and lives as gifts from God.

36. The Grass Is Greener under the Chicken Coop. 1. Answers will vary. **2.** A vain woman always feels like she deserves more than she already has. Her ego fuels her desire for more attention, more money, more kindness. She will never be satisfied, which is the exact opposite of how God wants us to live. **3.** Greed and lust are sinful appetites, but coveting is an action that colors your perception about your life. When you covet, you do not love your neighbor and you are not loving yourself. Coveting hurts you by persuading you to be selfish. Coveting hurts your neighbor because it leads to sin against them. Coveting hurts your relationship with God because you're ungrateful for His blessings. **4.** In Psalm 104, we see all the parts of creation that God maintains and sustains. We can trust God to maintain and sustain our lives in the same way. We don't have to covet what God has given anyone else. He takes care of each of us according to each of our purposes. **5.** Answers will vary.

Commandment Ten. 1. Answers will vary but will include women's stories and plans about how we can help protect one another against all the evil that threatens our homes, our things, and our relationships. **2.** Answers will vary, but women might say that social media and our society's consumerist culture encourage us to covet more. Coveting may be a more prevalent sin today than it was five hundred years ago or five thousand years ago.

37. Dying on the Inside. 1. Answers will vary. **2.** Answers will vary, but most women will talk about wanting success, money, more things, attention, and approval. The Holy Spirit sanctifies and changes our desires so we want more faith and relationships rooted in Christ. **3.** Jesus is exasperated that these men care so much about their own images but not about their own faith or need for a Savior. Like the Pharisees, we are often guilty of finding our value in what the world thinks of us, more than in our value as God's child. Our hearts are sick with coveting for what will make us look better. **4.** We see the theme of Matthew 15:21–28 repeated throughout the Gospels. Many times it's the weird rejects of society who have strong faith. We cannot judge who truly believes and who does not by how they look or how they fit into this world. **5.** Righteous fear is like awe, like an understanding of God's supreme power in our lives. In this way, fear is an important part of our faith.

38. Identical Notes to Fraternal Twins. 1. Answers will vary but will include that we often identify ourselves more by what we don't have than by what God has given us, especially when we compare ourselves to siblings or best friends. This takes our eyes off our own prizes and points our focus on our sister's blessings. **2.** Answers will vary, but most women will share how God has provided opportunities for them to use the talents He's given them. **3.** Coveting does not add up to unity in Christ; it creates division. When we're deceitful and greedy, we are like children, tossed around by every wind of doctrine. Instead, we should work together as one body, building each other up in love. **4.** Answers will vary, but women will tell stories about how they can see God molding seasons of their lives into fruit for His kingdom. **5.** Answers will vary.

39. Something's (Not) in the Water. 1. Answers will vary but will include testimonies of God's perfect planning for our fertility and our families. **2.** Answers will vary. **3.** Peninnah and Hagar were both prideful for what God had given them. Instead of seeing their babies as gifts, they believed they had earned their children and that they had earned God's favor. When we are arrogant, we proudly show off what we believe we've earned. **4.** God sent His Son through the birth of a baby in a stable in Bethlehem. With the arrival of this child, God adopted us as His children. We are no longer slaves to sin; we are His precious daughters. **5.** Answers will vary but will include that only the Holy Spirit can help you see God's love so you understand He is taking care of you in every single way and giving you what you need.

40. Crumbling the Caste System. 1. Answers will vary but will include that no one really understands another person's life. **2.** Coveting tells us that we are the "have nots" in the world. This is a lie because God provides richly for each one of us. Through our life stories, God gives us perfect blessings for each season. **3.** We all sin and fall short of the glory of God. Our pride constantly tells us not to admit this, to believe we are fine. We would rather believe in a caste system where success is in our control. In God's system of free grace, we have full access to exactly what we need, His love. **4.** God's love is the great equalizer. It's a lie to believe one soul is more valuable than another. When God sees us, He sees Christ in us. Because of this, He forgives and accepts us. For eternity, and for everything that really matters on earth, we are exactly equal. **5.** Answers will vary.

Appendix

THE TEN COMMANDMENTS AND THEIR MEANINGS

As the head of the family should teach them in a simple way to his household

THE FIRST COMMANDMENT

You shall have no other gods.

What does this mean? We should fear, love, and trust in God above all things.

THE SECOND COMMANDMENT

You shall not misuse the name of the Lord your God.

What does this mean? We should fear and love God so that we do not curse, swear, use satanic arts, lie, or deceive by His name, but call upon it in every trouble, pray, praise, and give thanks.

THE THIRD COMMANDMENT

Remember the Sabbath day by keeping it holy.

What does this mean? We should fear and love God so that we do not despise preaching and His Word, but hold it sacred and gladly hear and learn it.

THE FOURTH COMMANDMENT

Honor your father and your mother.

What does this mean? We should fear and love God so that we do not despise or anger our parents and other authorities, but honor them, serve and obey them, love and cherish them.

THE FIFTH COMMANDMENT

You shall not murder.

What does this mean? We should fear and love God so that we do not hurt or harm our neighbor in his body, but help and support him in every physical need.

THE SIXTH COMMANDMENT

You shall not commit adultery.

What does this mean? We should fear and love God so that we lead a sexually pure and decent life in what we say and do, and husband and wife love and honor each other.

THE SEVENTH COMMANDMENT

You shall not steal.

What does this mean? We should fear and love God so that we do not take our neighbor's money or possessions, or get them in any dishonest way, but help him to improve and protect his possessions and income.

THE EIGHTH COMMANDMENT

You shall not give false testimony against your neighbor.

What does this mean? We should fear and love God so that we do not tell lies about our neighbor, betray him, slander him, or hurt his reputation, but defend him, speak well of him, and explain everything in the kindest way.

THE NINTH COMMANDMENT

You shall not covet your neighbor's house.

What does this mean? We should fear and love God so that we do not scheme to get our neighbor's inheritance or houses, or get it in a way which only appears right, but help and be of service to him in keeping it.

THE TENTH COMMANDMENT

You shall not covet your neighbor's wife, or his manservant or maidservant, his ox or donkey or anything that belongs to your neighbor.

What does this mean? We should fear and love God so that we do not entice or force away our neighbor's wife, workers, or animals, or turn them against him, but urge them to stay and do their duty.

THE CLOSE OF THE COMMANDMENTS

What does God say about all these commandments?

He says, "I, the Lord your God, am a jealous God, punishing the children for the sin of the fathers to the third and fourth generation of those who hate Me, but showing love to a thousand generations of those who love Me and keep My commandments." (Exodus 20:5–6)

What does this mean? God threatens to punish all who break these commandments. Therefore, we should fear His wrath and not do anything against them. But He promises grace and every blessing to all who keep these commandments. Therefore, we should also love and trust in Him and gladly do what He commands.

For Further
Reading

- *Luther's Small Catechism with Explanation*, 1991 edition, Concordia Publishing House.
- *Luther's Large Catechism with Study Questions*, Concordia Publishing House.
- *Basic Bible Teachings*, Concordia Publishing House.
- *Lutheranism 101*, second edition, Concordia Publishing House.
- *The Christian Faith: A Lutheran Exposition*, by Robert Kolb, Concordia Publishing House.